DARING
TO DREAM

The Work of The Hope Foundation
in India

Ethel Crowley

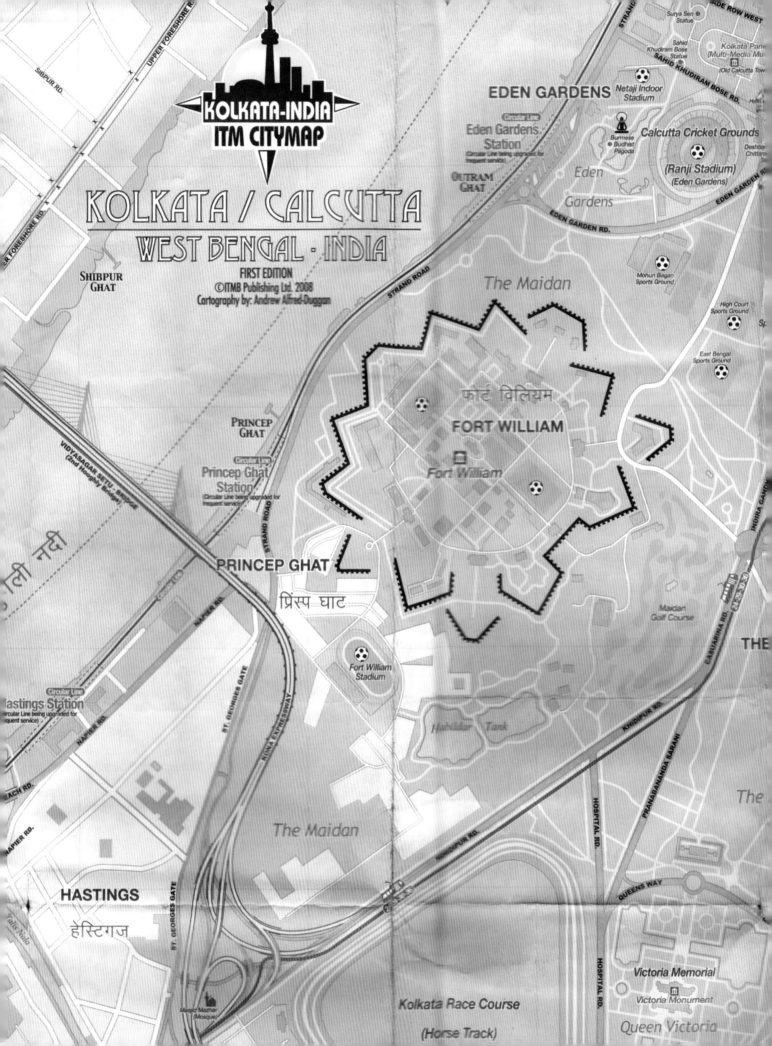

KOLKATA-INDIA ITM CITYMAP

KOLKATA / CALCUTTA
WEST BENGAL · INDIA
FIRST EDITION
©ITMB Publishing Ltd. 2008
Cartography by: Andrew Alfred-Duggan

SIBPUR RD.

UPPER FORESHORE R.

SHIBPUR GHAT

PRINCEP GHAT

VIDYASAGAR SETU - BRIDGE
(2nd Hooghly Bridge)

Circular Line
Princep Ghat Station
Circular Line being upgraded for frequent service.

PRINCEP GHAT
प्रिंस्प घाट

हुगली नदी

Hastings Station
Circular Line being upgraded for frequent service.

NAPIER RD.

BEACH RD.

NAPIER RD.

ST. GEORGES GATE

NUNA EXPRESSWAY

HASTINGS
हेस्टिंगज

Tolis Nala

Masjid Mazhar
(Mosque)

EDEN GARDENS

Surya Sen Statue

ADE ROW WEST
STRAND
Sahid Khudiram Bose Statue

Kolkata Pan (Multi-Media Mu (Old Calcutta Tow

Netaji Indoor Stadium

Circular Line
Eden Gardens Station
Circular Line being upgraded for frequent service.

Burmese Budhist Pagoda

Calcutta Cricket Grounds
(Ranji Stadium)
(Eden Gardens)

OUTRAM GHAT

Eden Gardens

EDEN GARDEN RD.

Deshba Chittara

Mohun Bagan Sports Ground

High Court Sports Ground

STRAND ROAD

The Maidan

East Bengal Sports Ground

EDEN GARDEN R

Sp

फोर्ट विलियम
FORT WILLIAM

Fort William

Fort William Stadium

STRAND ROAD

The Maidan

Maidan Golf Course

THE

INDIRA GANDH

EARHARINA RD.

PRANABANANDA SARANI

KHIDIRPUR RD.

Haldar Tank

KIDDERPORE RD.

HOSPITAL RD.

QUEENS WAY

The

Victoria Memorial

Victoria Monument

Queen Victoria

Kolkata Race Course
(Horse Track)

HOSPITAL RD.

First Published in 2010 by
The Hope Foundation,
3 Clover Lawn,
Skehard Road,
Cork,
Ireland.

ISBN 978-0-9567408-0-9

Graphic Design by Brendan Cotter
www.brendancotter.atspace.com

Printed in Ireland by Uppercase, Cork.

Cover pic - Ethel Crowley

Contents

Acknowledgements

Researching and writing this book has been an enormously satisfying project. To bear witness to HOPE's work in Kolkata was a great privilege. This team has shown me that nothing is impossible when you put your mind to it. Maureen Forrest and Jenny Browne are a fantastically dynamic pair of sisters who radiate positive energy and who could run a country if they were let! The team of Irish volunteers were a great source of support and fun. Annemarie Murray let me tag along on several occasions, and answered possibly hundreds of questions! I would also like to single out Gora Das, who was interrogated by me on a daily basis and who facilitated my research arrangements in Kolkata with grace and good humour. I would especially like to thank JP O'Sullivan, who was very supportive of me while I was completing the book. I wish to thank all HOPE staff who contributed to this project in various ways, including those who wrote the Annual Reports each year. These provided the structure for the book, around which I built my own research. I also want to thank Brendan Cotter for the beautiful work on the graphic design. All pictures in this book were taken by the author, unless otherwise stated. All proceeds from this book go directly to the Hope Foundation.

Ethel Crowley

Find the Hope Foundation on Facebook and Twitter

facebook

INTRODUCTION

> " I slept and dreamt that life was joy.
> I awoke and saw that life was service.
> I acted and behold, service was joy. "
>
> Rabindranath Tagore

WELCOME TO CITY OF JOY KOLKATA

Introduction

THE HOPE FOUNDATION, the Irish non-governmental organisation (NGO), works in Calcutta (now called Kolkata), where millions live in abject poverty on the streets and in some of the biggest slums in the world. Since Maureen Forrest set it up in 1999, along with her faithful team both in Cork and Kolkata, they have literally saved the lives of thousands of children. Her sister, Jenny Browne, is the Overseas Director who is the permanent Irish presence there. The Hope Foundation was founded with the primary objective of helping underprivileged children gain access to protection, education, healthcare and nutrition, which they would otherwise have received if they had been born into different circumstances. The children of Kolkata have been the main focus of HOPE's work.

The journey started on February 7th 1999 with the establishment of the Hope Kolkata Foundation. Since the area of work has increased over the years, the organisation has been working with partners to address various issues that directly or indirectly affect children. The Hope Foundation has been working for the marginalized population with the mission of sustainable development in health and education for children, adolescents and women in both urban and rural impoverished areas since then. Their vision is to improve the quality of life of the most vulnerable among the underprivileged population of Kolkata and other parts of West Bengal. The Hope Foundation is implementing a range of

Maureen Forrest, HOPE founder and Director and Jenny Browne, HOPE Overseas Director

programmes focussing on health, education, protection, gender, skill development, income generation and capacity building in different parts of West Bengal with its partner organisations. HOPE believes in a more comprehensive approach that is fundamental for holistic community development for children, adolescents and women.

Areas of work:
- Health
- Education
- Protection
- Gender
- Skill development
- Income generation
- Capacity building
- Research and documentation

At a Glance:
- Meeting people's basic needs
- Addressing people's rights through advocacy and networking
- Reaching people in great need
- Making long-term commitments through capacity building

Kolkata city centre, street life

HOPE's Partners:
1. Hope Kolkata Foundation
2. Society for Educational & Environmental Development (SEED)
3. Mayurbhanj Joint Citizen Center (MJCC)
4. HIVe India
5. Bhoruka Public Welfare Trust (BPWT)
6. Society for Indian Children's Welfare (SICW)
7. All Bengal Women's Union (ABWU)
8. Rehabilitation Center for Children (RCFC)
9. Paschim Banga Krira – O - Janakalyan Parishad (PBKOJP)
10. Jayaprakash Institute of Social Change (JPISC)
11. Arunima Hospice
12. Human Rights Law Network (HRLN)
13. Haldarchawk Chetana Welfare Society (HCWS)
14. Mohammad Bazar Backward Class Development Society (MBBCDS)
15. Society for People's Awareness (SPAN)
16. Iswar Sankalpa
17. Mukti Rehabilitation Center

This book is a celebration of the work done by the Hope Foundation, describing in detail all of their work in Kolkata and beyond. This is augmented by interviews with HOPE staff and with some of the young people whose lives have been touched by them. I also try to fill in the background to their work by presenting some of the key issues in Indian society in a series called 'Spotlight'. These are the issues that prompted the staff of the Hope Foundation to reach out and help impoverished children: child labour and trafficking, gender discrimination, the mechanisms of poverty and illiteracy.

When one analyses social issues in India, it is very easy to become overwhelmed by the scale of the problems one encounters. The huge numbers of pavement-dwellers and slum-dwellers can easily lead one to view them all 'en masse'. It is very powerful to focus instead on the stories of particular individuals and on how people can develop when given a chance. It is mind-boggling to think that many of HOPE's beautiful young people who are now happy, healthy and educated started life impoverished, living on the streets and with no apparent hope of escape. This is the lesson that I was taught by HOPE – that all you can do is start with helping one person and build from there. There is a Chinese proverb that says, "those who say something is impossible should not stop those who are actually doing it".

After the six weeks I spent with HOPE in Kolkata in Nov/Dec 2009, one of the ideas that remains with me is that HOPE expands and redefines the meaning of *family*. Most of us are lucky enough to be raised by parents who love us, and to be surrounded by a family that celebrates with us in the good times and supports us in the bad times. While cultural differences mean that family forms vary across the world, the sense of stability and human connection remains the same.

The families who live on Kolkata's slums and streets are under intolerable levels of stress. They have often been forced to migrate from destitution in the countryside of West Bengal, or from across the borders of Bangladesh and Nepal. They have to do anything they can to try to survive in Kolkata, including the most degrading and back-breaking work. The very poorest engage in rag picking or begging. There are often enormous personal problems like drug/alcohol addiction and domestic violence, and a whole range of serious health problems, perhaps even as serious as TB or AIDS. Pollutions levels are so bad that lung problems are endemic. Most are of course undernourished, perhaps not even eating a proper meal every day.

Understandably, it is the children of these families who suffer the most. They often have to forego their education to earn a few rupees for the family, and their life chances are severely curtailed as a result. Their health is compromised, they may be starving, and they cannot speak for themselves. They are the most powerless of all.

When HOPE enters their lives, hope enters their lives. Their needs are assessed, and anything they need is provided. Whether it is medicine, clothes, proper food, shelter, schooling or counselling that is needed, it is provided. And this can be a life-long arrangement. HOPE has reared many thousands of children by now. They are the only effective family these children have. While they may have a biological family who visit them, they cannot provide for them due to poverty, ill-health or other problems.

When you speak to Maureen, Jenny, Geeta or Pushpa about the children, they may as well be their own. They will tell you stories about each individual as long as you let them. Indeed, many Irish people may wish that they received as much unconditional love from their own parents, as the HOPE children get from their caregivers. When the children are educated, grow up and become independent, they are so proud of them. When things go wrong, they are heartbroken. The little shrine in the Girl's Home still bears the picture of one of the first boys they took in who, despite surgery performed in Ireland, sadly died from a heart condition.

Most of all, like any good family, HOPE brings dignity and a sense of autonomy to the children. The backgrounds they were born into might well lead to lives of poverty and discrimination. They might be looked down upon as embodiments of overpopulation that needs to be controlled. With the care and education that HOPE provides for these children, there is no reason that they cannot fulfil all of their dreams, and become active agents in Indian society in the 21st century.

We begin this journey with an interview with Maureen Forrest, HOPE founder and Director, followed by an introduction to the work of Paulami de Sarkar, HOPE's Projects Manager at the Kolkata office, and that of JP O'Sullivan, Projects Manager at the Cork office. We then move on to put their work with HOPE into context by describing the main points of recent Indian development and the persistence of poverty there. We then move on to describe the city of Kolkata and its very particular character.

Victoria Memorial, The Maidan, Kolkata

interview...

Maureen Forrest, HOPE Founder and Director

"People place enormous trust in you when they give you money"

The Hope Foundation is the brainchild of Maureen Forrest. When asked how this path of development work began, she replies that it all started when a medical missionary nun visited her school. She made a big impression on her, as well as another visit from an Aer Lingus stewardess. This covered both of the major aspects of her life – development work and travel. She knew she did not want to become a nun, so even at the tender age of sixteen, she enquired about becoming a lay missionary.

She was one of a family of twelve children, so "the caring and sharing starts the day you're born". Two of the twelve were mentally challenged also, so that added to the amount of caring that had to be done. Her mother is still hale and hearty, having passed her 90th birthday. Most of her sisters are nurses and two are nuns and teachers. As was the case in the sixties and seventies in Ireland, one of the few career options was to do a commercial course. Having done this, she then went on to work in insurance and moved to London and worked in a bank. She then applied to Aer Lingus and got a job as ground staff in Shannon Airport. Around this time, she started her life-long romance with Dick Forrest, who was a son in a neighbouring family back home in East Cork. She married him at 22 and settled down to family life on the farm back home.

Her domesticity at this time did not prevent her from keeping up an interest in global development issues, however. During the Ethiopian famine in the early eighties, her sister, Ber, who is a nurse, volunteered with GOAL. This was a time when "famine was brought into our sitting rooms for the first time on television". She then started fundraising for GOAL and raised up to £50,000 in Ireland. She couldn't go to Ethiopia because she had three children, Louise, Robin and Ricky, and other commitments at home. However, later, John O'Shea (GOAL Director) asked her to go to Somalia and she went for six weeks to work in the refugee camps there. "It was a horrendous place to be. You were dealing with gunfire every minute of the day". She recalls one incident where her camp was shot at and she remembers lying on the ground thinking "I don't want to die on my own in a foreign country". It was hard on her family at home because they literally didn't know if she was dead or alive, as it was virtually impossible to ring home from there. She says that she was a bit "traumatized" when she came home as it was just before Christmas and she found it difficult to focus on the ordinary tasks of buying presents and cooking the turkey.

She says that over the years, Calcutta was always on her mind, which she attributes to the work of

Mother Teresa. Then President Mary Robinson visited Calcutta in 1993 and John O'Shea invited Maureen to visit with GOAL. She was horrified – "it's the scale of it". She refers especially to the rickshaw pullers, who are "treated as animals". She compares it to the apartheid era in South Africa – "can people not see the injustice all around them?" After her experiences in Africa, she viewed the slums as refugee camps, because many of the slum-dwellers in this city are the descendents of those who were displaced by Partition and the creation of Bangladesh. She asks "how can India be called a democracy? It suits the west to call it that because they want to trade with it. They choose to overlook big issues like the trafficking of children, child labour, children who go missing, dowry issues and child marriage".

She then decided to come to Calcutta to volunteer with GOAL, who funds local partner organisations. She went initially for six weeks, working with CINI-ASHA (Child in Need Institute), where she met Geeta, whom she subsequently invited to work with her in HOPE. They set up schools in the slums, which was valuable experience for her. She learned that the key to the success of slum children's education was to involve the mothers in the education process.

After this, she then went to work in the emergency relief camps in Goma after the genocide in Rwanda in late 1994. It was absolute horror, with 350,000 people and cholera in the camps. She was there for five weeks. She found that talking about it with other volunteers helped her rehabilitation after she got home. She went round the schools throughout Munster sharing her stories. She also visited refugee camps in Swaziland on the border with Mozambique. All of this experience had a huge impact on her. Her experience of emergency relief taught her that she preferred the sense of continuity in development work, "where you can see a child progress".

She admits that Calcutta was still on her mind. She came back in 1998 with her daughter Louise and spent a lot of time with Geeta. They started to set up an organisation. They hired a solicitor to tackle the enormous legalities involved. One has to have an Indian board of the charity. HOPE Kolkata is a branch of HOPE Ireland like HOPE UK or HOPE Germany, but it is the implementing branch while all the others are fundraising branches. The initial goal was to run a home for 25 children and raise £25,000 a year to run it. It snowballed into the size it is now, taking in over €2 million a year and employing a staff of 774 on the last count. It grew into something much bigger than anticipated. They learned that the way forward was to take on partners and work with established ones with expertise in different areas.

Maureen says, "getting the organisation built up took a lot of planning. At the start, it was just all in my head, but before long the delegation has to start, and you need good dedicated and qualified people. You have to keep building, you have to get ready for the handover, and there's a natural progression. One of the big issues is maintaining standards." She continues, "it's lovely to see the flow, to have a structure to pass on". She thinks she will retire at 70, but, she insists, "I don't worry about that, sure I'm still a young one!" She sees herself as part of an extended family, and she is helped hugely by Jenny Browne, her sister, the Overseas Director who spends most of each year in Kolkata. Jenny is a Mercy nun who taught Home Economics in Waterford until Maureen asked her to work for HOPE. Jenny's degree in Social Science also informs the work she does with HOPE. She praises the team in Cork as well: JP, Madeleine, Eunice, Margaret, Sardar, Fiona, Susan, Rosaleen and Pauline. She likes having younger people on board, as for example, JP has set up "Next Generation Hope", a very successful Facebook online contact initiative.

Comhlamh sets standards for NGOs and audits for good governance systems and procedures. Irish Aid insists that they use a 4-pronged programmatic approach, using the MIS system, involving monitoring and evaluation. They have earned the trust of the Irish government. In their third year, the

Gujarat earthquake happened and HOPE appealed to the Irish public at home. Irish Aid funded HOPE because they had staff and expertise already in place. They have affected the lives of about 23,000 children in Kolkata: in crèches, coaching centres, clinics, but it could stretch to millions if you take into account Maureen's work on relief in Africa and in Gujarat and Tamil Nadu after the tsunami. The Indian government department on HIV has now asked HOPE to get involved in distributing a food programme, to use their expertise. All of these are very positive developments for the organisation.

Just for fun, I asked her why she does it, why does she not stay home and pay golf? She laughs, "I'd be so bored. I was always someone who needed to work. Now I'm fitting everything into the autumn of my years". She does admit, however, that "it can be lonely, people often aren't interested. You can see their eyes glazing over when you talk about Calcutta!" Her husband visited and he was "bewildered". He doesn't like cities in general, so Calcutta was a very extreme experience. He joked "I've been in Calcutta twice – the first time and the last time!" She says that he couldn't take the confusion and the filth of it, and understandably prefers to be home on his farm in familiar surroundings.

They are very committed to keeping the running costs of the organisation down. She takes no salary at all herself. Jenny, herself and Annemarie Murray (long-term volunteer) live at the top of the Girls Home in Panditya Place. The conditions are basic, and they live right next to the rescued girls in adjacent rooms. I asked her if she would she not think of getting an apartment in the city that would be more comfortable. Her answer: "no, I'd hate to move out, it would make me lose touch with the dynamic of the thing. My only concern is that we're using a room that children could be in". The building at Panditya is old, and there is a plan to build a new custom-built building that would make better use of space. They are still searching for the funding for this, however. HOPE has to work with local government to build new premises on any site. Sometimes having the money for the job isn't enough in itself, as there may not be the space to build in such a congested city. Hence they often have to use existing little rooms, in agreement with the local municipality or community. One school operates in a galvanised container that was sent from Ireland.

Keeping the funding coming in is the major priority. The team are very imaginative in coming up with new ideas. She has a doggedly determined spirit: "there's no such thing as a real no, there's always a way. There's always another source". They get no direct grant aiding from the Indian government, but their partners do, to various extents. They are starting to target private Indian donors now as well, since there is now more wealth in the country than before. She is thankful that they have not had to cut any projects like some other NGOs due to the recession, as she asks, "where would you start?"

She sums up their *modus operandi* like this: "it's all about trying to get as many children into education as possible, and as many women into work as possible". There is a clear focus on addressing gender discrimination. She has found so often that in any one family, the girl child is starved while the boy is fat and healthy. There is also a focus on educating mothers on their reproductive cycles, thereby contributing to women's empowerment. Education is the only way to achieve long-term success – coercion is not an option. So many of the women are illiterate that this can be difficult, so they focus on the use of condoms for contraception and HIV prevention, and tubal ligation for long term contraception.

For all its problems, she says "I love Calcutta. I love the people. They're very cultured. And I love the children, of course". She has passed on her love for Calcutta's children to her own family back home. Before Christmas, her three- year-old granddaughter, Emily said, "Santa is coming to me, but I'm giving some of my presents to your babies in India". Her picture is on the office notice board in Kolkata, on which someone wrote "Baby Director". Who knows? Maybe in twenty year's time, she will be the real Director!

interview...

Paulami de Sarkar Projects Manager, Kolkata

Paulami de Sarkar (B.Soc.Sc., M.S.W.) is very wise for her years. Despite being still only in her twenties, she is the project manager for 60 HOPE projects, implemented in cooperation with 16 local partners. She has been working here since February 2006, having completed her Masters in Social Work. Her job is comprised of managing all the projects, preparing quarterly reports for donors, writing funding proposals and sending them to the Cork office. There is a constant process of upgrading and professionalizing going on. She remembers the training she received at university, where one of her mentors said that one should always leave an organisation in better shape than one has found it. She feels that she has to "wear two hats", being an intermediary between the requirements of the MIS and the concerns of the social workers on the ground.

There are four streams in HOPE's work: health, holistic education, child protection and finally, income generation. She implements a Management Information System (MIS) for each stream, so all the partners have to follow the one project model. She sets monthly targets and the partners send in monthly reports to her. She holds monthly meetings to check how things are going, for example, if there are any problems meeting targets. The projects overlap and she allows flexibility between them all. She is training staff in the implementation of these new systems, and she also trains the partners in how to file reports to government. There is an ongoing process of capacity building and training in management skills. She has also written a best practice manual for NGOs.

Another part of her job is that she also monitors budgets, as she puts it, "project MIS needs to tally with financial MIS", and if there is any discrepancy she sees it, making partners accountable for their own budgets. She polices the budget part of new project proposals, which can be difficult. She says, "you have to be patient, but ultimately, you are providing a better service to the community". She has developed employee and volunteer policy and also mentors university students who come to do projects. She also organises events like the annual day for 700 Community Health Volunteers, a sociable day that "gives them a team feeling". She spearheaded the SOLAS campaign on child labour and she reckons the petition was very successful, which she will now submit to the Governor of the state.

Paulami is the organiser, the 'tough cookie' whom nothing gets past. She feels she represents the young generation, who are more business-minded and action-oriented. She says, "the crying days are over", meaning that it is not enough to be just concerned about the poor, but you have to set about helping them in a practical manner. She maintains professional managerial standards that would appear to comply with standards anywhere.

interview...

JP O'Sullivan, Projects Manager, Cork

"A small body of determined spirits, fired by an unquenchable faith in their mission, can alter the course of history"

(Mahatma Gandhi)

From Volunteer to Full Time Staff Member

JP O' Sullivan (B.Soc.Sc., M.S.W.) is a recent recruit to the HOPE team in Cork. In his late 20s, he has previously worked at Eason's book store, at the British Library in London, and he has also worked in mental health services in the north of Co. Cork. He signed up to volunteer with HOPE in Kolkata as his placement while studying for his postgraduate degree. He had worked with another NGO in India before that, so he had clearly been bitten by the India bug! He also had grown up hearing stories about Kolkata from his aunt's husband, who was born there. It was perhaps written in the stars, then, that he would eventually work in the city that formed part of his family lore.

He first volunteered with HOPE in September 2007 for a period of five months, and returned the following year for a further four months. He has had a further two six-week stints since then, so he knows the city very well indeed now. When he went there first, he feels that the support of both Indian and Irish staff was crucial to his orientation. He singles out Anne Marie Murray for special mention in this regard. He says that for him "it feels like home. People are very relaxed and friendly". He adds, "the city is chaotic, but the people on the streets control the chaos – they create their own worlds within it. At times is feels like each child doesn't know about the others and can seem hugely isolated as a result. They make their own way as best they can".

His current job with HOPE is a multi-faceted one. He writes funding proposals and donor reports, he administers Next Generation HOPE, he networks with youth groups and with third-level institutions, as well as providing orientation and support for volunteers. He was also part of the three-person team who wrote the document on HOPE's child protection policy, now a crucial aspect of every NGO's work. He always has his finger on the pulse, as he is in contact with the staff in Kolkata on a daily basis. He feels that he is working with a team who share the same vision and mission as himself, feeling honoured that he can be "an ambassador for change". He likes that every day is different, which keeps the job very interesting.

When asked why people should continue to donate to HOPE during the current recession, his response is heartfelt. He says, "the children on Kolkata's streets experience their own social and personal recession every single day. They have no platform, no voice, no-one wants to listen to them". He adds that HOPE provides them with education, encouragement, and the support to become the next policy makers - "there are no boundaries on their dreams". He wishes to acknowledge the support of every single donor and fundraiser, no matter what the amount. To donate €10 or €100 can be a huge sacrifice for some people - all acts of generosity are hugely encouraging. For example, he has just

The HOPE team at the Cork office

Madeleine Cummins, Manager/Network
Co-ordinator

The team at the Cork office

Fiona Heraghty,
Fundraising Projects & Volunteer Co-ordinator

Margaret Doyle,
Office Administrator

Eunice Tait, Accounts Assistant & Office
Administrator

Susan Forrest,
Marketing Co-ordinator

Alison O'Brien,
PR & Media Co-ordinator

Rosaleen Thomas,
Fundraising Director

Pauline Coffey,
Fundraiser

Serdar Suer,
Accountant

received an email from a 13-year-old girl, asking how she can help HOPE. He says, "young people are the future, and they don't receive enough recognition for the good work they do".

Even though he has met thousands of children in Kolkata, one child in particular is uppermost in his thoughts. Sabir lives on the streets with his parents. JP encouraged him to come to one of their centres for a few hours of art and recreation every day. One day, JP wrote something down, and Sabir corrected his spelling. JP asked him how his English was so good, and his devastating reply was "I need English to beg from people like you". This boy still lives on the streets, as the final choice in these matters has to stay with the families themselves. However, HOPE has encouraged him to express himself and "given him a chance to really be heard". This child can then ultimately "facilitate his own future". That is what the work of the Hope Foundation is all about.

Recent Indian Development and Poverty

The current phase of Indian economic development is generally deemed to have begun in 1991. This was the year when India's economy went bankrupt, the International Monetary Fund stepped in and radical measures had to be adopted to save it. Then Finance Minister Manmohan Singh initiated reforms to kickstart the economy. The new policies involved the abolition of the 'Licence Raj', the elaborate red tape resulting from the industrial licensing system. This opened India up for international trade and investment. This switching to an open market economy meant a whole new tranche of inward investment. India's annual economic growth rate since then stands at an average of seven to eight per cent per annum, which translates to about $200 billion a year, exceeding the total GDP of Portugal or Norway.[1] This new economic strength means that India is now being taken seriously as a player in world markets, as well as that other economic giant, China. As McMichael says:

> There is no doubt that the phenomenon of "Chindia" has the attention of the business community – whether as an investment opportunity or a threat to northern businesses or jobs.[2]

The sheer size of the population potentially makes it an enormous market for consumer goods like electronics and cars. The huge size of the economy is deceptive, however, considering that the purchasing power of the vast majority is extremely low, as we will see later. It is often quoted that the Indian middle class stands at about 300 million. However, western brands are still massively expensive even for this middle class, and it appears that many of them prefer to stick to more familiar and cheaper Indian brands. Observations during visits to Kolkata's shopping malls would seem to suggest that the fancy shops selling Nike sportswear, Tommy Hilfiger sweaters and Swarovski crystals are treated more like entertaining museums than places to part with hard-earned cash. After all, professional salaries are still comparatively low in India, with a top executive in an IT firm perhaps earning €20,000 a year. So to part with €150 for a pair of jeans would be the privilege of a very small minority. However, many more could afford Indian-made clothes that fit better both culturally and financially.

One sector that has grown massively since the nineties is Business Process Outsourcing, or BPO, as it is commonly called. This is the surreal world of call centres, in which nearly a million young Indians work. Adverts abound in Indian cities for schools where young people can learn 'BPO English'. Accents have to be US for US customers and UK for UK customers, because otherwise American and English callers think that a job has been taken away from their country. A call centre worker earns $50-60 for a 50-hour week, probably of shift work at night. Much of this work is in Bangalore and Hyderabad (also jokingly known as Cyberabad). It is high status work for Indian young people, and they can enjoy "a lifestyle that's a cocktail of premature affluence and ersatz westernisation transplanted to an Indian setting".[3] Travel writer Paul Theroux recently visited some of these call centres in Bangalore and was highly critical of what he saw as exploitation by both Western and Indian companies. He compared it to the coolie labour, which was the basis of the British Raj. He says that while this current workforce is intelligent and educated, they were nothing more than "cultivated coolies".[4] This judgement appears to be quite offensive to the young people who are making the best of their situation, and striving to get access to what little work exists for them. It is also perhaps increasingly factually inaccurate, as the range of services they provide expands:

Today, Indians are reading MRIs for American hospitals, running consulting services for global US firms, handling actuarial work for British insurance companies, analysing US and European company stocks for western institutional investors and writing software that will prevent Boeing and Airbus planes from colliding in mid-air. Hardly menial tasks.[5]

It is true, however, that the challenge of providing more decent employment for an expanding population is one that has yet to be addressed properly by the Indian state. These bubbles of a certain version of westernisation are but drops in the ocean of Indian unemployment and poverty. As respected writer Edward Luce says:

India's economy offers a schizophrenic glimpse of a high-tech, twenty-first century future amid a distressingly medieval past.[6]

Even the simplest of tasks requires basic literacy, so ensuring that the workforce is adequately educated for absorption into the formal economy is of premium importance. In 2010, official estimates are that one third of the population is still illiterate. One suspects that the real figure is higher than that. The fruits of economic growth cannot be shared without better access to such basic human rights. Nobel Prize winning economist Amartya Sen uses stark language on this subject:

The social backwardness of India, with its elitist concentration on higher education and massive negligence of school education and its substantial neglect of basic health care [leaves India] poorly prepared for a widely shared economic expansion.[7]

We have plenty of experience in the western world of the effects of long-term unemployment besides just that of low income. Sen outlines them for us: "psychological harm, loss of work motivation, skill and self-confidence, increase in ailments and morbidity (and even mortality rates), disruption of family relations and social life, hardening of social exclusion and accentuation of racial tensions and gender asymmetries".[8] In the western world, we have a tendency to dehumanise the poor of the developing world, to see them as just chronically poor, rather than as unemployed in the same way as we could be. The struggle to put food on the table for one's family is the same everywhere, just with the major difference that there is no consistent social welfare safety net in countries like India. If one cannot work, one can literally starve to death.

On the positive side, one revolutionary new feature of contemporary India is improved access to communication technology. The 'mobile miracle' has resulted from ending the 'License Raj', when the government lifted restrictions on business in the communications sector. One had to wait many years in the past to have a landline connected. There are still only 37 million landline phones in the whole country. Mobile phones are now in the hands of some of the poorest people, which must be a great source of empowerment and social connection. It is estimated that there are half a billion mobile phones in India now, operated by 14 phone companies. This represents 97 per cent market penetration in urban areas and 18 per cent in rural areas.[9]

The gap between rich and poor in India is about as wide as it could possibly be. There are a total of 48 Indians on the Forbes Rich List 2010, with industrialists Mukesh Ambani ranking fourth richest and Lakshmi Mittal ranking fifth, each with a net worth of about $29 billion. While this wealth creation no doubt creates some employment for those who can gain access to it, it means little to the vast majority. One of those on the Rich List, Nandan Nilekani, the CEO of Infosys, one of the most successful Indian software companies, is under no illusions about India's developmental goals:

The answer is not to send people back to the village, which anyway, you can't do in a democracy. It is to improve the quality of urban governance and to provide the poor with real jobs. The urban elites feather their nests with the best of comforts. Then they want to pull up the ladder and deprive everyone else of the same opportunities. Unless we start to provide the masses with jobs and increase the rate of economic growth, then everybody's security will be threatened. We have to embrace the future.[10]

It is also the case that even the rich, whether they like it or not, have to share in the inconveniences associated with the poor physical infrastructure one sees in most of India. Aside from the Golden Quadrilateral Highway, the new road connecting Delhi, Mumbai, Chennai and Kolkata, the quality of roads is generally poor. Even though the elite live largely sheltered and privileged lives, they still have to breathe the same polluted air, experience the same power cuts and travel on the same potholed roads as everyone else. As Paul Theroux says, "the biggest, fastest limousine is forced to travel at a crawl behind the pony carts and the skinny men on their bicycle rickshaws".[11] Sitting in a traffic jam in an Indian city, one bears witness to globally unparalleled extremes of wealth and poverty.

At the other end of the scale, UNICEF estimate that 42 percent of India's population lived below the international poverty line of $1.25 a day in 2007.[12] The health statistics are very stark indeed. Here are some examples:

- **India's current life expectancy rate is 64 years**
- **Over 50 per cent of India's children are malnourished, stunted and underweight**
- **25 per cent of deaths of newborn babies occur in India**
- **India's infant mortality rate was 52 per 1000 in 2008**
- **India's under-5 mortality rate was 69 per 1000 in 2008**
- **India has the highest number of child deaths in the world, caused by malnutrition of the mother and child, morbidity and disability**
- **28 per cent of infants have a low birth weight due to the poor health and nutrition of their mothers**
- **In 2008, only 39 per cent of Indian babies were born in a hospital or clinic**
- **The central government spends 14 per cent of GNP on defence, but only 2 per cent on health.[13]**

The definition of poverty is of course a very contentious subject. It is in the interest of the Indian state to minimise the numbers as much as possible. Official estimates are that 27 per cent of Indians are poor, defined as the monetary equivalent to consuming 1,900 calories a day. Back in the early 1970s, the officially designated poor were allowed 2,400 calories a day. By that definition back then, over half the population were poor. By gradually reducing the calorific threshold over the years, the

Indian state managed to massage the poverty statistics by shifting the statistical goalposts. By the standard of 2,400 calories a day, three quarters of the population are now below the poverty line.[14]

Moreover, going by the standard definition of a poor family being one that spends one third or more of its income on food, 95 per cent of Indian families are poor. If one uses the Chinese standard of a food share of 60 per cent, then about 70 per cent of the Indian population is poor. While 80 per cent of Indian households are calorie deficient, calorie intake is steadily falling. Food deprivation and insecurity persist on a mass scale. One half of the population is malnourished, and about 10 per cent severely malnourished. Children fare the worst. While 53 per cent of all Indian children are undernourished, 21 per cent are severely undernourished. Going by Body Mass Index (BMI), about half the population is chronically deficient. India has the world's largest malnourished population. Undernourishment among children is twice as high as in sub-Saharan Africa. A gigantic 40 to 60 per cent of Indian children are undernourished.[15] In 2000, one in five deaths in India was of an infant.[16] A new report has just been published revising the estimates upwards of those who are living below the poverty line. This study was led by economist Suresh Tendulkar. The previous official estimates were 27.5 per cent for the total population of India and 28.3 per cent for rural areas, but this report found it to be 37 per cent overall and 42 per cent in rural areas. This comes closer to the proportion estimated by UNICEF. Certain states like Orissa, Bihar and Jharkhand can boast that over half their populations are in absolute abject poverty. The revised figures result from defining poverty not just in terms of basic calorific intake as previously, but also in terms of broader education and health. Tendulkar recommends increased state spending on these sectors to try to improve the lot of India's poor.[17]

Most importantly, though, to define poverty solely in terms of calorific intake is extremely minimalist and misleading. This is just barely enough to stay alive, so maybe it should be renamed 'the starvation line' instead. It says nothing about other basic needs like health care, education, shelter, housing, fuel or clothes or indeed broader human rights. Just keeping people from actually dying of hunger seems to be the basic goal, thereby not attracting international attention. One author says that it "has been drawn just this side of the funeral pyre".[18] He goes on:

> To be poor is to be born of a malnourished mother in conditions where your survival is uncertain; to survive with inadequate food, clothing and shelter, without the stimulation of learning or play; to grow unequipped intellectually or physically to be a productive member of a striving society.[19]

The poor who live below the poverty line can apply to the state to get a 'BPL (Below Poverty Line) card'. This entitles them to subsidised rations of rice, lentils, wheat and sugar each month. While this is of course welcome, penetrating mind-boggling state bureaucracy if one is illiterate and destitute can be next to impossible. Also, anecdotal evidence from grassroots activists in Kolkata suggests that it can be difficult for the deserving to get access to a BPL card and some better-off people have them who do not need them. This extraordinary level of hunger and poverty exists at the same time as India is amassing huge stocks of food grain, so much that if it were distributed among the poor, each poor family would get one tonne each.[20]

It is clear that poverty needs to be defined in much broader terms than simply avoiding death. A state cannot be said to be caring for its people if services are not provided for them to try to rise out of poverty. Improved health care and universal primary education would be a very good start. Providing these services costs much less in India that it would in the west. Even these basic services would help poor people to try to create better lives for themselves and their families, and to have real choices in their lives.

One is poor if one does not have choices: if one has to work from a young age instead of going to school, or if one has to follow a life path that was chosen for them even before their birth, or if one is forced into early marriage and childbirth. None of these complex aspects of social life in India can be measured by rupees or calories, or indeed improved by money alone. There has to be a real political will to treat all citizens exactly the same, in practice as well as in theory, providing for all their needs regardless of class or caste. Economic growth is pointless and unjust unless attempts are made to ensure that everybody benefits from it. As Amartya Sen reminds us:

The basic point is that the impact of economic growth depends much on how the fruits of economic growth are used.[21]

With improved access to these services, healthy, educated and confident citizens can therefore become agents of their own destinies, rather than waiting patiently for the next crumbs to fall from the rich mens' tables.

The thorny subject that strongly affects this wealth distribution and makes Indian society unique is that of the caste system. While every society is unequal and divided to various extents by class differentiation and racism, the added issue of caste makes Indian society extraordinarily complex and extraordinarily hierarchical. This subject often makes educated Indians highly uncomfortable, but it is nevertheless a pervasive element of social life. Indians will still often mention which caste they come from when in conversation with new acquaintances.

In Hinduism, one is born into one of four castes and one cannot move up or down the hierarchy. This differentiates it from class, where either upward or downward mobility is possible, depending on one's fortunes in life. The four castes are firstly, the Brahmins, who were traditionally the priests and the learned, educated elite; secondly, the Kshatriyas, who were the noble warriors, or the defenders of the realm; thirdly, the Vaishyas, who were the traders, the businessmen, the farmers and the moneylenders; finally, the Sudras, whose function was to serve the other three castes as labourers and artisans. Outside of the caste hierarchy, literally 'outcast', were the 'untouchables', who performed demeaning jobs like human waste disposal and animal slaughter. Any association with them was traditionally seen as demeaning and polluting. To add to the complexity, there are also hundreds of sub-castes who are associated with particular regions of the country.

This regime has been in place for several thousand years. It is slowly declining in importance, but such hierarchical thinking is still strongly ingrained in the Indian psyche and evident in everyday life.[22] It is usually seen as essential to marry within one's own caste, in order to retain the ritual purity of the caste. Arranged marriages are still the norm, where parents decide whom their children should marry. Among the urban educated elite, however, one's education and earnings are usually now prioritised over caste, as it is quite common to see matrimonial ads in the newspapers proclaiming that 'caste [is] no bar'. Caste may be shifted to the back burner, but Varma argues:

"the new uncertainties – and opportunities – have only heightened sensitivities about who stands where in the pecking order, and only accentuated the obsession with status and power".[23]

The biggest liberator of the lower castes has been the process of urbanisation. When people are in close proximity on busy city streets, they cannot control whom they inadvertently touch or who cooks their food behind closed doors. The different castes are not immediately recognisable by sight, so people of different castes cannot really avoid each other, even if they so wish.[24] More overt caste hatred

Street scene, Kolkata

is visible in the rural villages, where, for example, an assignation between a boy and girl of different castes could well result in their deaths. One reads horrific stories in the newspapers every week about attacks of various kinds on low caste individuals. Apart from these extreme cases, many millions of rural dwellers are condemned to perform highly exploitative types of work simply because of the family, and hence the caste, into which they were born. Sometimes women are also sexually exploited because of their low caste status in their communities.

The Indian Constitution of 1950 outlawed caste discrimination. This was due to the input of Dr. Bhimrao Ambedkar, who, though not as famous as Gandhi, is just as important a contributor to recent Indian history. He was the principal author of the Constitution, ensuring that all citizens were deemed equal regardless of caste. Himself an 'untouchable', he rejected Gandhi's term for that group - 'Harijan' - as patronising, and instead coined the term 'Dalit', meaning 'oppressed'. He called this system 'an ascending scale of hatred and a descending scale of contempt'.[25] He led a mass conversion to Buddhism in 1956, as a means of escape from what he saw as the tyranny of Hinduism and an entry into a more egalitarian religious system. Statues of Ambedkar are common throughout India, standing as symbols of Dalit political consciousness.[26]

This political leader also ensured the initiation of the world's first affirmative action programme, where a certain portion of public sector jobs were reserved for the 'Scheduled Castes and Tribes'. These are comprised of Dalits, Adivasis or tribal people and 'other backward classes'. Together, 50 per cent of India's public sector jobs are allocated to these groups.[27] This programme has been radical by international standards, dwarfing the affirmative action programme in the US, for example. Lower caste regional political parties and leaders have emerged in recent decades. Their usual agenda appears to be to expand the system to acquire more power for their own particular group. This is hardly unique, of course, as India is not the only country where democracy has been hijacked by self-serving politicians. There is an Indian joke that says, "in India, you do not cast your vote, but vote your caste".[28] All over the world, we can witness ethnic identities becoming more, not less, important. With India's wealth increasing, one can only expect more power struggles over access to that wealth in the future.

Kolkata:

"Kolkata is more a state of mind than a city. It epitomizes all that is magnificent and all that is squalid about modern India: its people, its theatres, its coffee houses and its bookshops set against some of the most depressing slums, the most wretched pavement hovels, the most noxious pollution, the most irreparable decay in the world. It seems a city without hope, a soot-and-concrete wasteland of power cuts, potholes and poverty; yet it inspires some of the country's greatest creative talent. To the true Kolkatan there is no other city quite like it: if one tires of Kolkata ... one tires of life".

Shashi Tharoor (2007) The Elephant, the Tiger and the Cellphone p.371.

Calcutta has been synonymous in the Western mind with terrible poverty, and is usually associated with the work of Mother Teresa. Does it deserve its appalling reputation? Yes, but we must remember that parts of New York, London and Dublin are just as seedy and much, much more dangerous. It is extraordinarily safe for the visitor. When negotiating one's way around the city, while it is dirty, tough and crowded, one always encounters graceful good manners and a helping hand if required. The most fascinating conversations can be had with erudite ladies and gentlemen who visibly light up when you tell them you are from Ireland. Stories of the parallels between the two countries' independence struggles trip readily off their tongues.

Kolkata city centre

Calcutta was renamed Kolkata in 2000. This followed the renaming of Bombay to Mumbai, Cochin to Kochi and Madras to Chennai during the 1990s. Not everybody agrees with the rationale behind this and the old name is still used in common parlance. All of the city centre streets have also been renamed after Indian and international revolutionary figures like Gandhi, Nehru, Lenin, Ho Chi Minh and Mother Teresa. This renaming signifies that the old colonial days are over, and India is turning over an independent new leaf. In writing about the city, it feels right to call it Calcutta when referring to the colonial era and Kolkata when discussing the present.

Historically, Calcutta was a vitally important port city, having been established in the eighteenth

The graceful Vivekananda Setu, or the second Hooghly bridge, Kolkata

The Writer's Building, Kolkata. Seat of West Bengal government, which formerly belonged to the East India Company

century for the export of cotton to Lancashire and opium to China. It boomed throughout the nineteenth century and remained capital of the Raj until 1911. It was second only to London throughout the British Empire. The architectural remains of the Raj are still plainly visible, as the city is dotted with hundreds of enchanting old palaces. These are now nothing more than crumbling relics of another era, dominated by a thriving colonial merchant class. Many of those who made it what it was are now buried in Calcutta's Park Street Cemetery, often having succumbed to tropical diseases.

This city also views itself as the cultural capital of India. The stereotype of Bengalis is of a creative, passionate and sensitive people, personified in Satyajit Ray, filmmaker extraordinaire and J.C. Bose, esteemed scientist. It is the home of three Nobel Prize winners. Rabindranath Tagore won the Nobel Prize for Literature in 1913, adopted citizen Mother Teresa won the Nobel Peace Prize in 1979, and most recently, Amartya Sen took the Nobel gong for Economics in 1998. The spirit of the city is informed by intellectual debate, by poetry and by leftist politics. So Kolkata, whose name has been a byword for Third World poverty, is a mass of contradictions. That is what makes it so horrendously fascinating: reeking of poverty and pollution, but also reeking of character.

It has a rich and challenging history. Like other Indian cities, it was forced to absorb floods of refugees after the Bengal Famine of 1943-46, in the violent aftermath of Partition in 1948, the Indo-Pakistani War in 1964 and the secession of Bangladesh in 1971. Many millions live cheek by jowl. It is a multicultural city, where conflict between Muslims and Hindus is quite rare. One writer describes life there in the 1970s:

> *In the Kolkata neighbourhood where I lived during my high school years, the wail of the muezzin calling the Islamic faithful to prayer blended with the tinkling bells and chanted mantras at the Hindu Shiva temple nearby and the crackling loudspeakers outside the Sikh gurdwara reciting verses from the Granth Sahib. (And St. Paul's Cathedral was only minutes away).[29]*

It is also home to a large Chinese community, many of whom were prominent traders. This legacy becomes evident in the city's restaurants, where one is always presented with two menus, one Indian and one Chinese.

Things have changed over the years, though, and it is currently trying to reinvent itself as a thriving economic hub. Power cuts have not been as common since the early noughties as they used to be because so many of the major industries had left the city by then, reducing the pressure on the electricity power grid.[30] In the last few years, however, signs are emerging of positive changes, with the big new bridge, new roads, housing complexes, science parks, shopping malls and restaurants. In the midst of all the pollution and poverty, security staff guard all of these pristine new developments carefully, making sure that only the right kind of people can gain entry. This gives the city a schizophrenic atmosphere that is redolent of colonial times. This impression is exacerbated by the fact

that all of the old private clubs are still there, to serve the recreational needs of the city's elite.

This kind of wealth creation has little bearing on the lives of the pavement dwellers and slum dwellers, as hopes for the 'trickle-down' of this wealth are slim. Until there is more investment in primary education and health care, the life-chances of the poor will remain derisory. The gap between rich and poor is barricaded by illiteracy, malnutrition and poor health. However, at least, this kind of development does mean that Kolkata does not continue on its downward

Pavement dwellers

spiral, abandoned by India's cultural and political elites. With transparent and accountable leadership, it could offer opportunities to more of its citizens and readily solve many of the urban problems it currently experiences. In the meantime, the gaps are filled by NGOs like the Hope Foundation, providing healthcare, education, training and child protection to the abandoned citizens of Kolkata.

The extreme conditions endured by many locals are among the harshest on the face of this earth. Winston Churchill famously wrote in a letter to his mother "I shall always be glad to have seen it – namely, that it will be unnecessary for me ever to see it again". Even now, it really has to be seen to be believed. The poorest among the locals, like the rickshaw pullers, the rag pickers and the beggars, endure lifetimes of humiliating and backbreaking work to earn less than €1 per day. It is like somebody

Kolkata's rickshaw pullers, who have one of the hardest jobs in the world

Kolkata's rickshaws

has waged war on the poor, as they are forced to the edge of the cliff of survival. Pavement-dwellers build their shaky little structures with pieces of wood and plastic, and before long, they have become permanent. In many areas, one cannot walk on the pavements, hence one is pushed to walk out on the roads and risk life and limb among the traffic, composed of taxis, autos, cars and rickshaws (both human and bicycle). In Kolkata, everything takes place on the streets. There can be no secrets. All human life is here – you witness scenes that may be moving, shocking or enchanting. One thing is for sure – it is never boring.

The environmental conditions are among the worst in the world. The air is noxious, when dust from construction sites, belching car exhaust fumes, industrial emissions and smoke from street dwellers' charcoal braziers mingle in a poisonous choking cocktail. Respiratory diseases are rampant and the newspapers report on the 'PM count', i.e. the amount of particulate matter or dust in the air. The newcomer inevitably experiences a persistent nagging cough until their virgin airways get accustomed to it. It is like the whole city has had a heart attack, with its veins clogged by pollution and garbage. Most locals do not walk even a short distance,

A token attempt to control noise pollution!

but hop in an auto or taxi instead, since they are so cheap. So there is a vicious circle here – people do not walk largely because of the congestion and pollution, creating a demand for the automobiles that cause a large part of the pollution in the first place. It can take a long time to get from A to B, making the smallest job a major task. This is compounded by noise pollution from the constant use of car horns. There are some signs in the city centre discouraging their use: "Silence Zone – No Horn Please". Some efforts like this are being made by Kolkata Municipal Corporation. The metro has been running efficiently since its inauguration in 1984, rubbish is now gathered off the streets, and they are gradually introducing cleaner autos that are powered by liquid petroleum gas. Overall, however, Kolkata's sights, smells and sounds assault one's senses, staying in one's mind long after one has left.

Slum life

The hustle and bustle of life in a Kolkata slum

Kolkata: 'City of Joy'

If there is one book that one should read to learn about life in Kolkata's slums, it is of course Dominique Lapierre's *City of Joy* (1986). He conducted extremely thorough research, including actually living in the slum of Pilkhana for two years. While it is a work of fiction, it fills in Kolkata's social, cultural and political background meticulously. Its plot is woven around the fortunes of Hasari Pal, a migrant worker from Bihar, Stephan Kovalski, a young Polish priest and Max Loeb, an American doctor as they experience life in the City of Joy. It is extraordinarily factually accurate and an inspiring read.

The book was adapted into a film directed by Roland Joffe and starring Patrick Swayze and Pauline Collins. When they were filming it in Kolkata, there were lots of protests from local people, including even a bomb thrown on set. The protesters resented that foreigners should make a film depicting the horrors of poverty in Kolkata rather than showing it in a more positive light. They also said it was racist that an American had to be the main character. The prominent Indian writer Shashi Tharoor, however, disagrees with the censorship that these protesters represented. He says that Roland Joffe has as much right to locate his movie in a Kolkata slum as he himself has to write a novel set in America. This is redolent of the famous quote from Voltaire: I do not agree with what you have to say, but I'll defend to the death your right to say it". Also, it could potentially reach a much wider audience because it was made in Hollywood rather than if it was made by a more local or apparently authentic director.[31] Of course, comparisons can be made here with the protests against the more recent film *Slumdog Millionaire* and the Irish objections to the depictions of poverty in Limerick in Frank McCourt's *Angela's Ashes*. Nobody likes the camera to zoom in on the dark corners of their city's history and society. Despite this local opposition to the film, Lapierre is still a frequent visitor to Kolkata and West Bengal. Half of the royalties from the book and film have gone to a charity that he and his wife founded that supports the children of lepers. They administer the charity themselves from their Paris apartment.

Kolkata's street traders

This book is arranged according to the four main areas of HOPE's work. Chapter one deals with their work in health, chapter two looks at their holistic education programmes, chapter three focuses on their work in child protection and finally, chapter four highlights their work on gender issues, skill development and income generation. Interspersed throughout these chapters is a series called 'Spotlight' which forms a short introduction to the key issues in Indian society like population, child labour, trafficking and gender discrimination, among others. All in all, one hopes that the reader gets a good flavour of the work of the Hope Foundation and the unique place in which they work, what travel writer Paul Theroux calls "the mildly orchestrated free-for-all of India – something of a madhouse with a touch of anarchy, yes, but an asylum in which strangers are welcome, where anything is possible, the weather is often pleasant, and the spicy food clears your sinuses".[32]

[1] Tharoor, 2007a: 6.
[2] McMichael, 2008: 285.
[3] Tharoor 2007a: 17.
[4] Theroux, 2008: 222.
[5] Tharoor 2007a: 18.
[6] Luce, 2006: 59.
[7] Sen, 2000: 42.
[8] Sen, 2000: 94.
[9] Singh, 2009.
[10] Quoted in Luce, 2006: 59.
[11] Theroux, 2008:148.
[12] www.UNICEF.org
[13] www.UNICEF.org
[14] Patnaik, 2005.
[15] Sen, 2005: 212.
[16] Bose, 2006:174.
[17] Thakur, 2009.
[18] Tharoor, 2007b: 326.
[19] ibid.
[20] Sen, 2005: 213.
[21] Sen, 2000: 44.
[22] Varma, 2004: 19.
[23] Varma, 2004: 20.
[24] Tharoor, 2007b: 106.
[25] Luce, 2006: 14.
[26] Shah, 2004:124.
[27] Luce, 2006: 126.
[28] Luce, 2006: 14.
[29] Tharoor, 2007a: 63.
[30] Tharoor, 2007b: 310.
[31] Tharoor, 2007b: 314-317.
[32] Theroux, 2008: 146-7.

healthcare

The health care programme of the Hope Foundation aims to improve the health of the poor underprivileged members of society, targeting primarily women and children. In order to achieve this goal, HOPE is implementing different projects in West Bengal, working towards increasing access to healthcare facilities, improving water and sanitation facilities and improving health awareness.

1

Health Care
projects

PROJECT	PARTNER NGOS
Primary Health Care	HKF, HIVE, SEED, SPAN, MJCC, PBKOJP
Emergency Response Project	HIVe, HKF
Community Based Intervention for Homeless Mentally Ill	Iswar Sankalpa
Counselling for Mental Health	ABWU
Dance Therapy	ABWU
Observation & Screening Centre	ABWU
Hospital for Underprivileged Children	HKF
Rehabilitation of Orthopaedically Handicapped Children	RCFC
Hospice for HIV infected and affected children	Arunima Hospice

Millions of people live in overcrowded slums in Kolkata

I t is estimated that about one third of the population of Kolkata's 14 million people live in slums, with three-quarters of the Kolkata slum population living below the poverty line. The goal of The Hope Foundation's health care programme is to improve the health of the street and slum dwelling population within Kolkata and its surroundings. Reduction of child and maternal mortalities, the prevention of HIV, malaria and other diseases can only be achieved by creating a base of improved primary health care facilities and increasing the levels of health awareness of the underprivileged. Let us now address in the first of the Spotlight series one of the major issues that most people associate with India – that of population and high fertility rates.

"When motherhood becomes the fruit of a deep yearning, not the result of ignorance or accident, its children will become the foundation of a new race"

Margaret Sanger (1879-1966) American birth control advocate.

The population of India currently stands at 1.2 billion. It is projected to rise to anywhere between 1.3 and 1.9 billion by 2050.[1] About 27 million new babies are born every year in India. However, it is also an enormous country with enormous productive potential.

It seems to be a common-sense idea in the west that 'overpopulation' is India's biggest social problem. There is an underlying racism and prejudice here, transforming people into 'populations'. When people are viewed as 'populations', they are seen as excessive, superfluous and as objects that can be controlled and limited. The real concern that proponents of this idea have is with the social composition and the proportion of poor people in the population, rather than the overall numbers. There needs to be an increased focus put upon making sure that everybody has a chance to rise out of poverty and become a productive member of society. The focus on so-called 'overpopulation' diverts attention away from more crucial issues like the poor distribution of wealth in Indian society, the blinkered model of development that is prevalent and the meagre proportion of state funds spent on health and education.

There is no direct causal link between high population density and poverty and hunger. For example, China has only half the cropland per person as India, yet Indians suffer widespread hunger, while the Chinese do not. Taiwan and South Korea each have only half the farmland per person found in Bangladesh, yet nobody speaks of overcrowding in each of those countries. All throughout Africa there exist areas that are underpopulated, despite common perceptions. Japan and the Netherlands are among the most densely populated countries in the world, and also among the richest. Distribution of population is also important. The overcrowding is much worse in big poor cities like Kolkata than in rural areas, but the people at least have access to more services, social networks and information. They leave the countryside because they are pushed out by poverty, and they may have other family members in the cities who encourage them to migrate as they have. This of course leads to the inexorable growth of global slums in which people have to live in very rough conditions.

Instead of attempting to unscramble the riddle of which causes which - poverty or high population - I will argue that the best approach is to see both as having the common cause of powerlessness.

If we look at the past of western industrialised countries, we can see that fertility declined in Europe and the USA as a result of the following factors:
• The industrialisation of their economies decreased dependence on child labour
• Improved health provision lead to lower infant death rates
• Better opportunities were provided in the workplace for women and men
• Finally, the availability and use of birth control.

So the history of these western countries shows us that poverty and high population growth result in societies that deny security and opportunities to their citizens, where adequate land, jobs, education, health care and financial security are beyond the reach of most people.

The impact of the women's movement in Europe and the US also meant that women's voices were heard in society. The struggles for gaining the vote, access to employment, equality in the workplace and contraception were invaluable for improving the life chances of not only women but men and children as well. It is imperative that societies are adequately democratic to allow dissenting and protesting groups to become part of political discourse. In this way, people can make informed choices and form new sets of values in their lives, especially relating to fertility.[2]

There is no doubt that fertility rates are generally higher among poorer people. All of the following reasons for this fact derive from a lack of social power. The following are some of the main reasons for high fertility rates in India:

- Women's powerlessness to control their fertility means that they are forced into early marriage, leading to more years of child bearing and ultimately bigger families. A vicious circle emerges where the combination of economic necessity and traditional attitudes towards women's roles as homemakers and child bearers drives girls into arranged marriages at the age of perhaps 15, so they might have their first child at 16. Of the married women in India today, 75 per cent were under 18 at the time of their marriage, despite the fact that this is illegal. Childbearing takes a huge toll on women's health in India. Fewer than half of all Indian births are assisted by trained midwives or doctors, compared to 97 per cent in China.[3] A horrifying statistic is that for Indian women, there is a 1 in 70 chance of pregnancy- and birth-related death.[4] The logical conclusion of this argument, then, is to increase the power women can exercise over their lives by making education and job training available to them. When they have other options for their lives, they feel more secure financially, and this leads directly to decreased fertility. Access to contraception is important as well, in the meantime, as it were.

- Poor families often rely on the labour of their children, so they are seen as a financial asset, rather than as a liability as in the west. In India, as in other poor countries, one of the main human rights denied to individuals is the right to a childhood. Children are often a source of work and income both on the land and in cities from perhaps as young an age as four or five (see Spotlight 4).

- People see children as provision for their old age. In the west, we have social welfare support for those who need it, including the elderly. In the absence of financial state support for unemployed and elderly people in India, people have to fall back on their families to support them. This is directly connected to the Indian issue of the preference for sons. A father and mother of many sons accrues high status in their community. This is largely because of the thorny issue of dowry, which is a major burden on the parents of daughters. Despite the fact that it is technically illegal, they have to start saving from when they are born for their dowry when they get married. Also, daughters become part of their new family on marriage, so they do not provide for their own parents. Discrimination against girls is endemic in India (see Spotlight 7). Indian parents generally like to have at least two boys – an heir and a spare. So they usually will not use contraception or agree to be sterilised until this has been achieved.

- High infant mortality rates have been found by the WHO to be a major factor in increasing the fertility of couples. If they feel that some of their children will not survive, they are quick to try for another. In societies where violence, poverty and disease are endemic, larger families are a form of social insurance. When children's health is improved and they are more likely to survive, people see that they need to have less of them.

From this review of reasons for high fertility, it becomes clear that the only really feasible means to slow population growth is to instigate far-reaching economic and political change that will convince the poor that social arrangements outside of the family will provide them with adequate security and job opportunities. Poor women also need to be adequately educated to make informed decisions on contraception, so that they themselves can control their use without coercion. Badgering the poor or forcing them to use contraception without taking into account their real concerns about financial insecurity is ineffective and unjust.

The public health scheme that is available in West Bengal is called the Janani Suraksha Yojana (Mother and Child Protection Scheme), commonly called the JSY scheme. It is an attempt to encourage good practice among mothers and to be sterilised after they have had two children. The mother has to be over 18 for eligibility and financial support is given for the first two children. They are given blood tests, monthly check-ups, and ante- and post-natal care. They are given Rs. 500 before the birth and if they follow through and have their papers in order, they are given Rs. 100 after the birth if they go for post-natal check-up. If the birth is normal, it costs around Rs. 1,500 to have a baby in hospital. This could cost about Rs. 10,000 in a private hospital, which is well beyond the bounds of the poor. If babies are born in hospital, they will at least have a birth certificate. Many of the poor are never officially registered, meaning that their human rights can be denied as they go through life. Men are also paid about Rs. 500 to be sterilised, but take up for this is slow. Also, oral contraceptive pills (OCPs) are subsidised, costing only Rs. 3 for a month's supply, and 10 condoms only 1 rupee! They have to have the will and the confidence to go get them, though, from hospitals or NGOs. They are then encouraged towards having a tubal ligation after two children. This scheme ties sterilisation into a scheme that looks after women and children's health in an integrated fashion.

Overall, at the end of the day, each person has to do the best they can for themselves in harsh societies like India. Decisions on birth, contraception, abortion, and the distribution of resources involve a series of economic, political, social, religious and cultural influences at individual and social levels. They are not abstract statistics, but real people making decisions in particular social contexts. It has been found elsewhere that the best means of reducing fertility is educating girls and women and getting women into the labour force. As Amartya Sen says, " young women have a strong reason for moderating birth rates, and their ability to influence family decisions increases with their empowerment".[5] Fertility rates have declined substantially in the south Indian state of Kerala as a result of improving women and children's health and education, without recourse to any form of coercion. Expanding women's freedom to learn and work is the single best solution to the problem of high population growth.[6]

The following six sections outline the trojan work being done by HOPE to try to solve some of the health problems of Kolkata's poor.

Primary Health Care Project

T his focuses on improving the basic health status of poor families through fulfilling the following three objectives:

1. The provision of accessible and equitable curative and emergency health support through 35 healthcare clinics, both static and mobile, in different parts of Kolkata and Howrah.

3. Preventative health support through awareness generation and formation of up to 51 Community Health Groups. These groups have been trained on health issues, as well as on advocating their rights for themselves, thus becoming the health monitors of their own communities. HOPE conducts various awareness and sensitisation camps on health issues such as reproductive child health, seasonal illnesses, communicable and non-communicable diseases, HIV/AIDS, adolescent sexual health and drug compliance. It also facilitates the improvement of reproductive child health care for women and children.

3. The construction and maintenance of drinking water and sanitation facilities. The project emphasises improving the accessibility of safe drinking water and sanitation to ensure a healthy environment.

This project aims to empower the community with information that will help them to bring a positive change to their everyday practices.

HOPE defines primary health care as:

Socially appropriate, universally accessible, and scientifically sound first level care provided by a suitably trained workforce. Primary health care should be supported by integrated referral systems and in a way that gives priority to those in most need, it should maximise community and individual self-reliance and participation and include collaboration with other sectors.

This definition encompasses the World Health Organisation's (WHO) Declaration of Alma Ata (WHO 1978) and the recent Primary Health Care: A Framework for Future Strategic Directions (WHO 2003).

The health project was originally conceived through the observations of Hope Foundation partners on the health status of street and slum dwellers. The HOPE partners involved are Hope Kolkata Foundation, SPAN, SEED, PBKOJP and MJCC. They conducted research through focus group discussions and baseline surveys to discover the real needs of the communities they served. The research found that there are a number of factors contributing to the poor health of the street and slum communities:

- Overwhelming poverty
- Limited access to clean drinking water
- Lack of proper sanitation
- Lack of basic hygiene
- Close living conditions spread communicable diseases
- Migrant nature of this population
- Extreme climatic conditions
- High illiteracy rates
- Poor knowledge on what healthcare services are available and
- Limited access to healthcare services available.

The HOPE ambulance, with staff (l-r) Ali, Anup & Ganesh

Unloading container of drugs for use in public health clinics

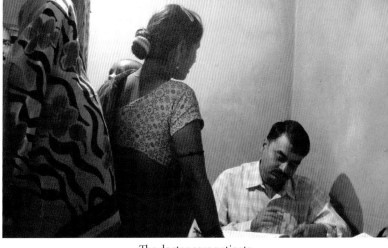

People queue up to see the doctor at a clinic.

The doctor sees patients

All of these factors render even pre-existing government services inaccessible to these communities, and as a consequence, the basic health needs of these people have not been met, and enormous suffering has become the norm for many thousands of people.

One of the major factors contributing to the low health status of street and slum dwellers is directly related to their low level of health awareness. Poor hygiene standards and malnourishment are affecting people's ability to fight off sickness, and poor drug compliance and low levels of immunization ensure that the communicable diseases are rampant in the slums and on the streets. The lack of knowledge on reproductive and sexual health is leading to a rise in sexually transmitted diseases (STDs). The high numbers of home births and low levels of antenatal and postnatal care among the city's poor has a terrible impact upon the health of mothers and children.

The Primary Healthcare Project is now running in its third year. HOPE runs seven clinics, while they co-operate with other partners (HIVe, PBK, SPAN, SEED, MJCC) to run the rest of the total of 35. Supported by Irish Aid, this programme spans across 34 street and slum communities. The aim of this project is to provide additional services to strengthen the existing health services being provided by the government of West Bengal. It has been found that networking and advocacy building results in improved accessibility for people to existing government health services.

1. Healthcare Clinics

HOPE aims to bring basic healthcare and healthcare awareness to the slum-dwelling and street-dwelling populations through these clinics. They will thus become more aware of other facilities provided by NGOs and Government-run healthcare institutions.

HOPE and its partners are now running 35 clinics in these communities. The clinics have provided quality health care through the diagnosis, treatment and medication of over 60,000 patients. Women are steadily becoming more aware of their own health rights. They have started taking care of their own health, and this is reflected in the number of women attending the clinics. Women and children are the primary focus of the programme.

The nurse dispenses drugs

The following is a profile of illnesses among Kolkata's poor:

ILLNESS	ADULTS	CHILDREN	TOTAL
Respiratory infections	7,580	9,763	17,343
Tuberculosis	58	41	99
Cardiovascular infections	2,932	55	2,987
Malnutrition	766	711	1,477
Gastrointestinal infections	7,311	5,195	12,506
Skin diseases	5,714	6,346	12,060
Gynae/obstetrics	3,398	95	3,493

Within the year 8,538 patients have been referred to government run healthcare institutions by the doctors and nurses, 6,787 of which were adults, and 1,751 children. Social workers have developed a good and effective rapport with these health institutions. The health staff also follows up on all the cases referred.

Extract:

India is home to many of the world's most polluted cities. The air in Calcutta or Delhi is all but unbreathable in winter, when exhaust fumes, unchecked industrial emissions, and smoke from countless charcoal braziers in the street rise to be trapped by descending mist and fog. A French diplomat friend, undergoing a routine medical check after serving three years in Calcutta, was asked how many packs of cigarettes he smoked a day. When he protested that he had never smoked in his life, his doctor told him to try another excuse; three years of breathing Calcutta air had given him lungs resembling a habitual smoker's. A visiting Australian environmental official told a Calcuttan friend that if Brisbane reached a tenth of the Bengali city's pollution levels, every factory in town would be closed down. As a result of such unchecked pollution, respiratory diseases are rife in urban India. Factories belch noxious black clouds; effluents pour untreated into rivers; sewage systems reek and overflow. ... A 1996 World Bank study estimated that air pollution killed more than forty thousand people annually in the six Indian cities it had surveyed, including 7,500 in Delhi alone. ... With respiratory illnesses, cardiovascular diseases, and lung ailments all caused by pollution, the total health costs for the country resulting from illnesses caused by pollution were estimated at 340 billion rupees ($9.7 billion), some 4.5 per cent of India's Gross Domestic Product. Ecologist Anil Agarwal looks at these figures starkly: they mean "that the entire economic growth for the year is being wiped out and development has taken place solely at the expense of the environment".

Shashi Tharoor (2007)
India: From Midnight to the Millenium and Beyond (pp.290-292)

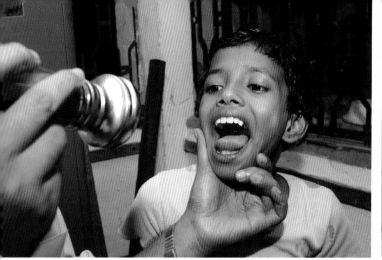

Say Aah! [Picture: Provision]

Doctor consults with patients at roadside

Madhumita Panga, a nine-year-old girl was found near Howrah station by a social worker of a partner organization working in the area. She was found on the roadside with her father, a migrant worker. She had been injured when she was six years old, losing her eyesight. As the family is very poor, they never took Madhumita to a doctor. The social worker who had spotted her asked her to come to the Howrah clinic where she was given some initial basic medicine and referred to a government hospital. After talks with the father to inform him of the situation, the girl was sent to Howrah hospital. At Howrah she was again referred, this time to Calcutta Medical College and Hospital, which renders specialized hospital services to all. She was seen by a specialist consultant, who advised that Madhumita should not only be admitted to the hospital, but also treated free of cost. After a successful operation Madhumita regained her eyesight. After three years of nothingness she was yet again able to see the world around her. A BPL certificate was applied for on her behalf, entitling her to medicines free of charge. Madhumita is currently in good form and is being followed up by the social worker.

Tumpa Mondol, a 22 year old female resident of Chetla lockgate area came to the clinic of one of HOPE's partners seeking treatment for her baby. The social worker noticed she had a shaved and bandaged head. After initial talks with Tumpa it was discovered she had suffered from a brain tumour four years previously. The tumour had been operated on at that time and doctors advised that she should stay in a government-run institution. Her family does not have enough financial assets to pay for medication, let alone the cost of a nursing home, so they brought Tumpa back to Chetla with them. From closer check-ups it was found that Tumpa was suffering from worms around the area of her head where she had had surgery. After repeated requests from clinic staff that she should again be admitted to hospital, her husband finally agreed and she was admitted to Chittaranjan Hospital. The social workers have been following up with the hospital and the Hope Foundation has paid for her medication.

Observation notes:

Annemarie Murray from Kilkee, Co. Clare is the Medical Co-Ordinator of the Primary Healthcare Programme run by HOPE in Kolkata's enormous slums. Her work makes a massive difference, bringing services to the doorsteps of those who could not otherwise afford healthcare. Annemarie and her team go to the slums every day in their small ambulance, a Maruti Suzuki. They visit each area on a three-week rotation, and the doctor is available once a week in each area. She is accompanied by a nurse, the driver and a healthcare worker who keeps the huge numbers of files organised. The staff works very well as a team, competently setting up shop either in small rooms in the slums, or out of the back of the ambulance. The room that I saw in Bandarpatti slum is very basic, the size of a small garden shed, about 4m x 2m with a bamboo roof. One of HOPE's partners, ABWU, runs an education programme here, and they approached HOPE to set up a clinic, which they duly did.

Annemarie Murray prepares for a clinic in a Kolkata slum

They set up at 11am, people queue up, show their red ID cards and get a queue number and come back after the doctor arrives at 11.30am. 30 people were seen the morning I was there. It was mostly women and children, as men are out working during the day. Clinics sometimes run in the evenings to try to reach the men. This slum is very close to main streets of city centre, right under the sign for the Hotel Royal Garden, one of the city's comfortable hotels. But it is a world apart, with its teeming humanity living in abject poverty. Some of the sights and smells include lots of baby monkeys chained to concrete blocks, reeking drains, rancid piles of rubbish being sorted for recycling and clouds of smoke from cooking braziers that catch in the throat. They keep meticulous records of the patients' ailments and drugs dispensed. The ailments are mostly respiratory (coughs, colds), gastrointestinal (including dysentery), skin infections (including scabies) and musculo-skeletal pain from wear and tear, which flare up especially in the cold of winter. They dispense relatively basic medication like paracetamol, cough syrup and antihistamines, but they do give out antibiotics too. The patients often get iron tablets, calcium and vitamin tablets, to supplement their meagre diets. Many of the slum dwellers are malnourished, which is why the midday meal at school is so important. The nurse instructs patients on how to take the drugs. Most are illiterate so they draw a diagram (eg. o|o|o is 3 a day) as to how many times a day to take them. They have to be careful to cut up the packets of tablets and break the seals on bottles, as there is a roaring trade for prescription drugs in the slums and they could be sold on. Certain brands of cough syrup have been abused by addicts too, so they have to be careful with that in particular. They try to advise them to use the government hospitals to avail of official government schemes, e.g., against TB and malaria. It can be very hard to get them to go, though, as these people are mostly illegal. When they have their babies, they try to get them to have them in hospital, so that the birth will be registered and the baby will have a birth cert. Some of the younger women do go, but the older mothers are more likely to have them at home in the slum. A baby had died recently here during a home birth. There is only one CHV here today. In this area, it is particularly difficult to get them involved, especially the men. The CHV that I meet is a forceful middle-aged woman. Some of them are more active than others, and they won't necessarily be there on clinic day.

They also hold public awareness sessions in the slums on various topics like nutrition, hygiene and reproductive health and contraception. In the latter, they would be female only and a lot of the Muslim girls wouldn't be allowed to go to them by their fathers or husbands. To reach the men, have to get to them in the evenings, and female social workers are reluctant to go out at night in the slums.

Annemarie Murray chats with some patients at a roadside clinic

2. Health Awareness and Community Health Groups:

The Hope Foundation is continuously strengthening the voice of its partner organizations through regular funding as well as facilitating advocacy meetings and workshops.

At local level, this programme empowers its Community Health Groups (CHGs) to improve health-seeking behaviour in its community. This is achieved through conducting health awareness events and camps at least once a quarter and through its efforts to improve the health of households in its community each year.

At national level, the CHGs participate in development through organising their events to coincide with the Government National Health Days, e.g. National Aids Day. This has a two-tier effect, in that the CHGs and communities become aware of what the government sees as its health priorities, and it also helps the government to reach more people than before. In effect, this component of the project bridges the gap between slum dwellers and government and ensures both are working side by side to improve the health of the poor.

Each CHG consists of twelve Community Health Volunteers (CHVs), four adult males, four adult females, two adolescent girls and two adolescent boys. Each group is trained and monitored by a qualified social worker. The CHVs are trained on the same topics as are targeted through the awareness camps and campaigns. They have been provided with intense and effective training on basic hygiene, nutrition, drug compliance, immunisation, first aid, seasonal illnesses, sexual health and reproductive health. Social workers have conducted regular awareness camps and campaigns in collaboration with the CHGs in order to increase awareness and sensitivity to these issues in the community. While this training has had a wide-ranging effect in the community, it has been found that a greater number of females attend awareness camps and training sessions than males.

Each year, there is a significant rise in numbers from the previous year and show that as people are becoming more aware of health issues and their primary health rights, they gradually start taking a stronger interest in supporting their communities. Healthcare is a basic human right and HOPE supports the CHGs in educating their communities. This is done through events and campaigns organized by CHGs, involving the community and helping slum dwellers gain access to already existing health services provided by the government.

One of the major issues the CHGs work on is based around reproduction, and social workers visit households to ensure complete antenatal check ups and post-natal check ups. These visits are designed to educate expectant mothers about care needed during pregnancy and possible danger signs. The *Janani Suraksha Yojona* (JSY) scheme provides women with antenatal and post-natal care and support. The incorporation of the JSY into the health awareness component of this programme has greatly improved women's realization that healthcare is a human right and as such is available to them. JSY camps have been organized to motivate pregnant women to deliver their babies in hospitals, and to minimize maternal and infant mortality through regular check ups in government institutions. Efforts are being made to form motherhood groups that can encourage the young pregnant mothers to access these facilities.

3. Water and Sanitation

In terms of supporting communities to gain access to resources for local development, HOPE collaborates with the Kolkata Municipal Corporation (KMC) to involve the communities in identifying existing needs for water and sanitation facilities. Water and Sanitation (W&S) committees have been created and are working with local councils for the maintenance of new and existing facilities. This not only ensures communities have access to resources, but is a good tool for local development and generating basic health awareness. Thirty three new latrine systems and eight new tube wells were constructed in different slum areas in 2008/2009.

Also:

As well as the three major goals outlined above, the Hope Foundation also puts a lot of energy into networking with the Health Departments of West Bengal. A good working relationship with government-run institutions is vital to HOPE's work in Kolkata. The following are examples of some recent positive outcomes, which make a major difference to the lives of Kolkata's poor:

- In Chetla area, it was found that the HOPE clinics coincided with those of Calcutta Rescue (CR). Clinics at Chetla were thus terminated, as the government of West Bengal funds CR, and it is a more sustainable option to keep CR for their clinics.

- A blood donation camp was organized with Bhoruka Blood Bank who specializes in such events and is funded by the government, so if any crisis occurs, blood will be available in the communities.

- Networking with the Calcutta Lions Bimal Poddar Eye Hospital resulted in free eye check ups for people in Banderpatti and Bedford Lane. 219 were diagnosed with eye problems, most of which were given special discounts on spectacles and those with cataracts were operated on.

- Networking with Manipal Health Systems resulted in a cardiac camp for children in Panditya.

- In Mothertala, an unregistered slum, inhabitants do not have a recognized address and as such cannot seek government identity cards. In light of this, it is almost impossible for pregnant women to avail of the JSY scheme. Advocacy conducted with the Borough office has resulted in them providing a special form for inhabitants which ensures that even though they do not have the relevant documentation, they can still benefit from the scheme. The CHVs are responsible for helping people fill out these forms and will be able to do so long after the completion of this programme.

- The organization intervening in the Mothertala area has worked to identify partially immunized children and contacted M. R Bangur Government Hospital, who are now providing vaccination for these children.

- KMUHO are a government sponsored healthcare provider with a specific remit in the area of immunization. KMUHO was encouraged to hold a general health clinic in Basanti colony after HOPE highlighted the need in this locality. Through follow up visits it had been learnt that the people of this community are now actively availing of this healthcare facility.

- In the Nareldanga area, one of the partners has identified and motivated twenty youths to take part in an initiative by the Kolkata Police Authority: Green Police. The aim of this programme is to involve local youths in maintaining law and order in their communities. The youths have received training from Kolkata Police and may also have the opportunity in the future to join the police force. This initiative gives the youths status within their communities and a voice within a civic body.

- Due to advocacy meetings held by a HOPE partner, the Integrated Child Development Supervisor (ICDS) in one area expressed her wish to co-operate in future activities like the immunization of children, mid-day meals etc. Now the organization identifies the malnourished children within the community and sends them to the local ICDS where they are provided with the regular mid-day meal.

- HOPE has also developed an effective partnership with ICDS centres. There are many poor patients identified with TB within the community. The organization helps the patients to get regular Direct Observation Treatment (DOT) from government hospitals and HOPE works with ICDS centres to provide nutrition to patients who are suffering from TB and are under DOT treatment.

- The Primary Health Care team of one of the HOPE partners was invited to an Eye Donation Seminar at the premises of the Sambhunath Pandith Hospital, with the objective of networking with the local civil society to eradicate blindness.

Geeta in the HOPE ambulance doing the night run in the city
[Provision]

83 Cent
is the average annual cost per person of providing a street or slum dweller with access to healthcare in the HOPE Primary Healthcare Clinics.

This project aims to provide emergency health care to those people who are poor, distressed and in need. The Emergency Response Unit (ERU) responds to people in crisis and in any need of physical or psychological emergency response and support. It runs 24 hours a day, 365 days a year. This project includes the rescue of abandoned children, trafficked children and women, people who have been involved in traffic accidents or mentally ill people who live on the streets. Psychological support is provided to people if required, as well as hospitalisation and treatment in cases of poor and homeless people. The service also includes repatriation of rescued victims of trafficking and follow-up support for them.

Another component entails developing an effective networking and referral system. It works towards networking between the local police stations and hospitals and rehabilitation centres. The project responds to the emergency calls from the police, fire brigade and clubs and other key stakeholders. The project is running successfully under all 48 police stations of Kolkata police and district, and West Bengal police stations around Kolkata.

The HOPE ambulance is "a beacon of light", says Maureen Forrest. Over the past year the ERU responded to 426 emergency calls, out of which 388 cases were followed up further. Seventeen homeless mentally ill people were sent to rehabilitation homes for psychiatric treatment. Out of 222 cases hospitalised, 133 were restored back with their families, 40 were placed with rehabilitation centres/halfway homes, and finally 16 people are still undergoing treatment at hospitals.

There is a separate Crisis Intervention Unit for girls and boys. Here they provide support to the rescued children and provide them with emergency treatment, after which a counsellor is brought in to work with the child. The challenges faced with this project are ongoing and include:

- Rejection from hospitals
- The indifferent attitude of the police
- Difficulty in placing people who are experiencing poor mental health, due to the scarcity of proper rehabilitation centres
- Hospital authorities take a long time at the time of hospitalisation
- Refusals from government restoration centres whilst trying to place senior citizens into their care.

Hope Kolkata Foundation runs its own ambulances, conducting a night run seeking out people in need of help. All of the staff takes turns on the night run, so they all become familiar with the areas where the poor congregate, and even with particular individuals.

It also works on this emergency response project with HIVe, one of its local partners.

interview...

Nitai Mukherjee, Secretary of HIVe

Nitai is an omnipresent figure driving his ambulance around Kolkata's streets. Emergency response is HIVe's priority. Their philosophy is to rescue children first: as Nitai says, "walk the walk first, then talk the talk". HIVe has existed for twenty years. At its inception, it was hoped that it would be "a hive of initiatives". It started as a non-violence movement to prevent the government from demolishing the slums. They put their bodies in front of the bulldozers, and lobbied on behalf of slum-dwellers to allocate some land for housing.

This developed into a service whose priority was to deliver emergency care to the street and slum poor. The Child Watch programme started with the night patrol "to fill the gap between services". He has literally thousands of stories. For example, he brought a girl from the streets in a traumatised state to Panditya Girls Home, and rescued a woman who had been nearly killed by her husband. Rejection from the hospitals is a common experience because of the pressures on the health system. He also finds that "the mindset of the people in the health system is often found to be not sensitive enough to the rights of citizens".

The people on the streets are migrants from the surrounding area, especially from the Sundarbans (a very poor delta region south of Kolkata), lost or homeless mentally challenged individuals, destitute, runaway, sick, abandoned persons including women, adolescents and children, survivors of domestic violence and also those who have suffered financial disasters. HIVe provides "a thin line of hope, some one to hold their fragile hands with care and dignity". Nitai explains:

"While patrolling the streets every night we have move very slowly, keeping all our senses fully alert, making sure that nothing going wrong and no one is at risk. Food packets are given to the people who are found to be starving. Often fellow street dwellers inform us about the other ill people on the street, who are taken to the hospital there and then. They are also instrumental in providing us with valuable information about lost, runaway or trafficked children, women and senior citizens suffering from neglect. Almost every night we get calls from Kolkata police and we respond immediately. It may be a call for rescuing a child being trafficked or sick or found runaway or a woman victim of domestic violence. We find some of the sick patients rotting with maggot-infected wounds on their bodies. After giving primary care and dressings we have to remove them to the HOPE hospital, because no other hospitals admit these patients. Almost one third of our rescued patients suffer from mental illness. Sometimes they are found in absolute quietness or some times in violent moods. We also have to respond to the accident or disaster calls from the police and fire department".

In the city by night, the street people are visible because they have the space to themselves. Nitai says, "it can be a place of torture and even death for people who have no roof over their heads". They started to build networks and to gain the trust of the street people. Some of them now have mobile phones, so that has turned them into stakeholders. They can send a missed call to him or to other social workers and they will then respond accordingly. Nitai feels that families living on the streets have become more confident and feel protected because of regular visits from the Night Watch team. These street dwelling people now act as "extended hands of the Night Watch Team" as they themselves reach out to some unknown children, women or elderly persons at risk.

Most importantly, the attitude of the police has changed a lot over the years. They have learnt to accept street dwellers as part of society. In hundreds of cases the police played a significant role in attending to their problems along with the Night Watch Team. They chip away at the prejudices of the police too. They reported one junior policeman for extorting money (Rs. 280 a month) from poor pavement-dwellers. While this is equivalent to only €4, it might be almost a week's wages to Kolkata's poor. He told them that since they paid no rent, they had to pay rent to the city and he was their landlord. His boss reprimanded him and made him sit at the metro with a begging bowl like a street beggar. HIVe does notice a change in the attitude of government employees, as they try to change their biases and prejudices. Nitai reports that they have a good relationship with the juvenile court. They serve as advocates for the poor to increase their awareness of their rights.

The influx of people into the city never stops. He says that, on a personal level, the amount of distress they come across day and night is enormously depressing, but on the other hand,

"we learn about the untold, unheard suffering of our fellow brothers and sisters. Our hearts get a kick and get us rolling. The challenges are taken up and some positive differences are made every day and night. Be it in sunlight or in the darkness, our people, our children, our mothers – they live under the bare sky. We need to be there 24/7 because they are our fellow citizens".

3

The Rehabilitation Project for Orthopaedically Handicapped Children

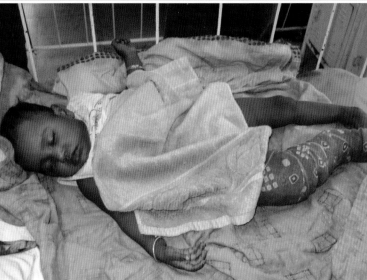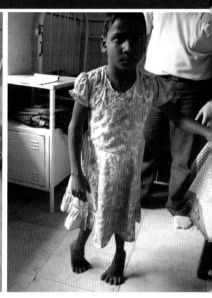

Left: Sundeep doing his rehabilitation exercises Centre: The children have one leg fixed at a time, about 15 days apart
Right: Sampa, who has Bilateral Equinus Foot

This project runs clinics for poor orthopaedically disabled children. It provides specialised assessment, surgery, physiotherapy and hospital treatment to children with orthopaedic conditions. It also offers artificial limbs, aids and appliances and fittings, according to the needs of these children. In order to achieve this goal, HOPE funds some of the work of Rehabilitation Centres For Children (RCFC).

This rehabilitation centre for children has been up and running since 1973, when it was founded by a British nurse and social activist, the late Jane Pamela Webb. It began with funds from a German philanthropic organisation, and grew steadily over the years. It developed into an institution that can provide free comprehensive rehabilitation for sixty children under the age of 14 from underprivileged families. Surgery is performed on a voluntary basis. On average, about 32 disabled children are operated on each month at the Barisha facility.

The main mission of RCFC is the comprehensive rehabilitation of orthopaedically handicapped children aged 0-14 years. These children are from underprivileged families in Kolkata and surrounds, some rural areas of West Bengal and the neighbouring states of Jharkhand and Bihar. The fundamental approach of RCFC is to give emotional support to physically challenged children along with surgery, treatment, physiotherapy, artificial aids and appliances, and imparting formal and informal education. This multi-dimensional approach is probably not available under the one roof anywhere else in India.

RCFC Services:

- A hospital with 22 beds for corrective orthopaedic surgery
- A residential block that can accommodate 75 post-operative children
- A Mobility Aid workshop for making prostheses and orthopaedic equipment
- A school for residential children, so that they can keep up with their school work while under care
- Pre-vocational training facilities
- Physiotherapy and cerebral palsy units with modern equipment
- Psychosocial rehabilitation

They also carry out *identification camps*, *follow-up programmes* and *awareness generation programmes* in the villages and rural areas of West Bengal and adjoining states. In 2008/2009, fourteen campaigns and nineteen Early Identification camps were conducted. They also have a field unit at a nearby town, Bolpur, for a clinic every Sunday. The camps and awareness programmes provide these communities with access to appropriate rehabilitation services at RCFC, and generate better health awareness. Such camps involve the family, community and the service providers. Through such interactive discussions they are able to generate awareness highlighting the importance of health. RCFC has worked in co-operation with the local bodies to make the scheme successful. In fact, the campaigns and camps have been a great success, and are fully backed up by the local bodies who have demanded that more camps and campaigning take place in their areas. In its 35 years of hard work, these are some of its achievements:

Dr. Mahendra Kumar Sahoo, surgeon at RCFC

- 63,000 patients assessed in its Out Patients Dept
- Over 10,000 operations performed
- Almost 16,000 mobility aids distributed
- 20,000 children covered under the immunisation programme
- 42,000 patients benefited from physiotherapy
- Over the past year RCFC had 735 beneficiaries (old and new patients), performed corrective surgery on 219 children and worked with 257 sufferers of Cerebral Palsy.

The most common complaint is 'club foot' or CTEV (Congenital Talipes Equino Varus) or Talipes Foot. In 2007/2008, they treated 123 cases of club foot with great success. Between December 2008 and April 2009, 56 out of 176 cases assessed in their Out Patients Dept had CTEV, and 37 had Cerebral Palsy. Sixty per cent of CTEV cases are bilateral (both feet) and they operate on one leg at a time, with fifteen days between operations. The reasons for the prevalence of this condition are unknown, but poverty and resulting poor antenatal care seems to be a contributory factor.

Many children also suffer from osteomyelitis, Koch's Disease of the bones and joints, and old fractures that didn't heal properly. The children often have severe deformities, and the surgical and therapeutic staff of RCFC strive to ensure that these patients do not leave until they can stand straight and walk, either with or without artificial appliances. Dr. Sahoo is the permanent physician on the premises who cares for the children throughout their stay, as well as being the surgeon. There are also six visiting doctors who work on the children.

This child has had her left foot operated on, with the right one next to be done

> **RCFC operate a sponsorship programme where:**
> - An operation costs $800
> - Care for a child for 1 year costs $500
> - Education of a child for 1 year costs $250

4

The Polyclinic and Hospital for Poor Underprivileged Children in Kolkata

HOPE Hospital

"The HOPE hospital is a miraculous place, bringing life back into dead bodies"

Nitai Mukherjee, Secretary of HIVe

This hospital was set up by the Hope Foundation to provide quality care and treatment to the deprived and destitute children from Kolkata and the surrounding area. It specialises in preventative health check-ups and round the clock quality care and treatment, thereby catering for all the health needs of these children. There is a holistic approach at the hospital, incorporating the preventative, curative and rehabilitative aspects of children's health.

The HOPE Hospital was funded by Weight Watchers Ireland, both North and South, a project spearheaded by Rita Fagan. Their impressive fundraising earned €350,000, and they also committed to supporting it for its first five years. It is now running in its third year, open since Nov. 21st 2007, and officially opened on Apr. 15th, 2008. At its inauguration, Maureen Forrest stressed that the hospital had not been established to duplicate any existing services, but to provide a place to treat children who face rejection at other healthcare centres. While health care in Kolkata is improving, it still provides services mostly to those who can afford to pay for it. This hospital aims to bridge that gap in services.

The four-storey hospital's in-patient services include 30 beds, 15 in the male ward and 15 in the female ward. Of the thirty beds, twenty-two are reserved for children and eight for underprivileged adults. They perform almost every kind of surgery in their operating theatre. Specialised doctors and nurses are on hand to provide constant supervision of patients. It employs forty staff, comprising non-medical, para-medical and medical skills. Both in-patients and out-patients can all gain access to sixteen different specialist consultant doctors, including in the following areas:

- **Paediatrician**
- **General Medicine**
- **Cardiologist**
- **ENT Specialist**
- **Gynaecologist**
- **Orthopaedic Specialist**
- **General Surgeons**
- **Dermatologist**

There is a Medical Officer on call twenty-four hours a day, seven days a week who employs thorough admission procedures. Poor patients avail of the services from the hospital's out-patients department, giving them access to basic healthcare that they would otherwise not be able to obtain. The vast majority are rescued off the streets, many of whom have been refused admission to government hospitals.

There are particular medical challenges associated with dealing with destitute people from the streets. Firstly, the need for their services is huge, and there are often not enough beds for the demand that exists for them. Secondly, it can be difficult for doctors to take a thorough medical history. The patients may have no information on their pasts and probably have no other contact persons. For instance, there may be old injuries or allergies that the medical team does not know about. Thirdly, they have to deal with destitute adults who have nowhere else to go. The CEO of the HOPE Hospital is Samiran Mallik (M.Sc.). He says that he always gives the best treatment possible, that HOPE "never say no, they never compromise on treatment".

Samiran Mallik, MSc. (Biochem), CEO of the HOPE Hospital.

Dr. Aniruddha Maitra (general medicine)

Dr. Ajoy Ghosh (general and paediatric surgeon)

The hospital also has a fully equipped pathology department; a qualified team is available, including an experienced pathologist, biochemist and laboratory technician. To date, tests for blood sugar, haemoglobin, blood group, lipid profile, cholesterol, triglycerides, billirubin, AST and ALT have been performed for patients. The hospital also contains an x-ray department equipped with modern instruments, a qualified radiologist and technicians.

Achievements:
- 152 patients have been admitted to the hospital In-Patient department
- 46 patients have gone through specialised surgeries and treatment in the hospital
- 4,041 patients have been provided with treatment through the Out-Patient Department
- 2,441 patients have received pathological tests
- 205 patients have received ECG
- 781 patients have used the X-ray facilities
- The hospital has organised 19 Immunization Camps for children, including children suffering from HIV/AIDS.

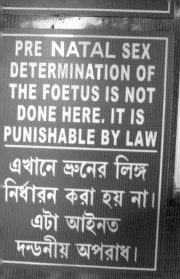
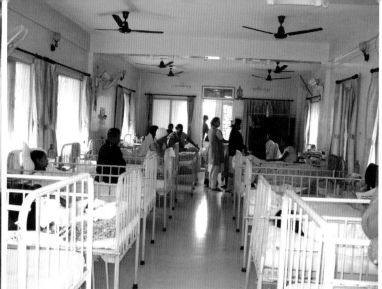
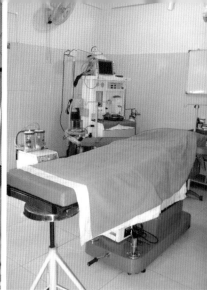

Left: The use of amniocentesis for the determination of the sex of the foetus is now common among pregnant women in India. It is illegal, as its purpose is to abort the foetus only if it is a girl. This plaque is in plain view at the hospital's front door.
Centre: The female ward in the hospital. Right: The operating theatre

Success Story!

Little S. (two and a half years old) came to the attention of the HOPE hospital via an email from another NGO in the area. She is from Paharpur village, in the interior of West Bengal. Since birth she has been suffering from the rare condition Hirschprung's Disease, characterized by the inability to pass waste matter through the bowel and out through the rectum. Within her two and half years, S. had been operated on twice to create a temporary pathway through her stomach to channel out waste from her bowel. She needed to undergo the final, complex surgery to artificially create a healthy passageway from her bowel to her anal canal and rectum. There were no facilities in her immediate area where she could have this important surgery done. She was then referred to an eminent surgeon, who agreed to do the surgery, but at a cost of Rs. 40,000, which her family could not afford. Her father works as bread hawker and the monthly family income is Rs. 1,500. The family therefore survive below the poverty line. An appeal was made to HOPE, and they immediately brought her in to the hospital, where the life-saving surgery was performed successfully, free of charge to her family. She made a full recovery.

Success Story!

A mother of 35 years and her two daughters of 7 and 8 years were rescued from the street by the HOPE Night Watch team. They were all victims of the common infectious disease, chicken pox. While this disease is not serious in the West, it became very serious for these poor pavement-dwellers. They were living in dire poverty suffering from severe malnutrition. This combined with their inevitably unhygienic living conditions and their lack of education, meant that their case was extremely severe by the time it came to HOPE's attention. They had been denied treatment in a government hospital. Their lesions became severely infected after being scratched, and all three had big deep wounds on their scalps that had become infected with maggots. In the heat of the summer and the polluted atmosphere of the city, wounds take a long time to heal. The filth of their living conditions led to their infections. They were admitted to the HOPE hospital in April 2009 after being refused by all Governmental hospitals. They were treated with IV antibiotics, and the wounds treated with ether and super oxides. They all made a full recovery.

5 The Mental Health Project

This deals with the mental health problems of individuals, affecting all facets of one's life. Therefore an all round effort is necessary to prevent long term mental health issues. The key focus is identifying and treating the disease as early as possible. Since the children and young adults come from very vulnerable backgrounds, they are often highly traumatised and resist any form of communication. It was found that rehabilitation is impossible without psychological therapy. Thus HOPE offers intensive counselling to the children who are in need of care and protection. It runs a one-year training course in psychological counselling for the caregivers of the shelter homes in order to improve the childcare practices in the homes. Since many children have learning difficulties, the organisation has started an observation and screening centre to assess their learning capacities and to provide specialised support.

Community Based Care and Treatment for Homeless Mentally Ill Patients:
There are an estimated 400,000 homeless people with poor mental health in India. This project also offers treatment, rehabilitation and repatriation for this group. They are often seen, in various states of mental distress and physical abuse, around railway stations, bus stands, pilgrim centres and on street corners. They are some of *the invisible people*, often separated from or neglected by their families. Nine out of ten of these people have diagnosable and treatable mental disorders. As a result of the lack of available treatments and services, Mukti Rehabilitation Centre started Project *Naya Daur* as a community based care and support programme for the homeless mentally ill in Kolkata. The specific focus of the project for the period was to initiate the care and treatment of the beneficiaries of the project, mobilize community resources and simultaneously continue with the baseline survey and community resource mapping for the care and treatment of the patients.

Challenges faced on this project:
- The mobile nature of the patients
- The lack of a mobile mental health unit
- The lack of community motivation and responsibility
- The absence of family members willing to provide support
- The poor physical conditions of mentally ill patients means that the project has to take care of patients' general health needs first
- A complicated legal process is required to ensure the admission of a patient to a government mental hospital.

Activities:
- Identifying, treating and repatriating 300 homeless mentally ill people
- Providing emergency hospitalisation for fifty patients
- Providing essentials like food and clothing
- Running two Drop In Centres for mentally ill people
- Follow-up on patients.

Counselling Project:
This is a special counselling training unit and observation and psychometric testing for the children. The Counselling Programme aims at providing special support to destitute traumatized children in difficult circumstances, who are residents of the Children's Welfare Home. The overall objective of the project is to ensure proper rehabilitation and mainstreaming of the children and young girls of the Children's Welfare Home.

Dance Therapy: Dance for Healing, Self-Expression & Rehabilitation:

Many of the children coming to the Children's Welfare Home have experienced severe trauma, a substantial number are mentally challenged while several require psychiatric treatment. These children do not benefit from traditional counselling. In most cases they do not have the ability to understand or benefit from talking to a counsellor as they lack the facility for normal reasoning. It was therefore decided by experts that non-traditional forms of counselling must be provided for these children. Dance therapy is one of the methods used to counsel the special children who are unable to follow regular methods of therapy.

Observation & Screening for Improving the Mental Health Status of Children:

The Children's Welfare Home provides housing to children who mainly arrive from government shelters and homes via Court directives and also through the Juvenile Justice Board. Many of these children are suffering from mental traumas due to conflicts or abandonment by their families. These are the main factors responsible for the children's personality and behavioural problems, and the focus of rehabilitation strategies. The Observation and Screening Centre uses a panel of psychiatrists, counsellors and psychologists to whom the cases may be referred. The Advisory Body consists of three psychiatrists, three counsellors and three psychologists. Their reports help to create a rehabilitation plan for the children.

HOPE PARTNER: ISWAR SANKALPA

Iswar Sankalpa is a non-profit organisation based in Kolkata, founded by professionals from the field of psychological well-being. They extend support, provide professional guidance and ensure sensible and sensitive services for the needs of the mind. Their team comprises psychiatrists, social workers, psychologists and activists who work with the community, hospitals, homes and shelters to bring acutely needed medical treatment to those homeless people suffering from psychological disorders.

Vision:
To ensure the dignity and holistic well-being of persons with mental health problems.

Mission:
- To lend a helping hand to those with mental health problems, particularly to those from underprivileged sections of society, and to do so in a humane manner
- To empower mental health patients in attaining their rights.

Their work involves:
- The identification and assessment of homeless mentally ill persons living on Kolkata's streets
- Providing medical treatment, hospitalisation and follow-up care
- Rehabilitation of the homeless person, either by restoring them to their families, or by re-integrating them into the community.

Their **treatment and care delivery model** involves utilising all the resources available to them, including Kolkata police, the government health and welfare departments, the media, other NGOs and community-based organisations, and last but not least, the patient's family and broader community.

Naya Daur (The Dawn of a New Era)

This is the flagship project of Iswar Sankalpa. It is a sustainable community-based care and support programme for the homeless mentally ill. These people are often treated as social pariahs, instead of people with treatable illnesses who deserve respect and equality. This is a programme that weaves together the state, the private sector and the community sector into a network of resources that not only cares for the beneficiary population, but works actively towards making them productive members of families and communities. In a resource-scarce environment, the community model has proven to be cost-effective, by using infrastructure and services already available within the state, other NGOs and private citizens. In this way, they have been able to support a larger number of beneficiaries than if they had followed a conventional institution-based approach. Between 2007 and 2009, they treated 200 patients and provided food, clothes and hygiene care to hundreds of others. They also organised awareness camps on mental illness in communities and advocacy meetings with the various institutions involved in dealing with patients.

Spotlight 2: HIV and AIDS in India

There are estimated to be currently about 2.4 million people living with HIV/AIDS in India. It is very difficult to gather accurate statistics, however, as some states provide none at all. Malaria and TB are much more common diseases, but treatment needs to be available for all the problems people can have.

It has been found that women and children are becoming increasingly vulnerable to HIV/AIDS. Currently about 39 per cent of infected people are women, indicating the increasing feminisation of HIV and AIDS in India. This alarming trend is being observed closely, as more HIV+ mothers will unknowingly pass the virus on to their children. India has an estimated 220,000 children infected by HIV/AIDS. It is estimated that 55-60,000 children are born every year to mothers who are HIV+. Without treatment, these newborns stand an estimated 30 per cent chance of becoming infected during the mother's pregnancy, labour or through breastfeeding after six months. This is termed vertical transmission.

The number of AIDS cases in the state of West Bengal is estimated at 23,640, among these no less than 3,000 children who are in dire straits and in need of anti retroviral therapy (ART). Of these, only about 15 per cent are currently under care, and a miniscule percentage is on ART. Proper nutrition is also crucial for these children, to improve their long-term chances.

Those children affected by HIV and AIDS through the illness and/or death of a parent suffer terrible trauma and hardship. They often become even poorer by losing their rights to the family land or house. These children not only lack money, but basics such as food, shelter and medical supplies. They do not know how to protect themselves and have poor access to health care facilities. These children are deprived of their childhood, facing economic hardship, providing care to their ill parents, and taking responsibility for other siblings and older members of their family. These affected children are forced to take the role of elders. Many unsurprisingly fail to cope with the situation. Society fails to ensure the rights of these children who deserve care and love. The stigma associated with HIV creates further social problems for these children, as in some cases they may be excluded from normal activities in their communities.

Children of patients play on the slide
[Kelly Campbell]

The HIV/AIDS hospice, called Arunima (meaning 'ray of the sun'), exists since June 2006, but HOPE's funding of some of its activities is very recent, only beginning in late 2008. It is the only AIDS hospice in Kolkata and surrounding district. It is a community care centre, caring for over 30 patients who are either infected with HIV and AIDS or affected by the virus, in that one or both of their parents are living with it. Ten of the beds are reserved for children and mothers. HOPE funded the construction of an extra ward for women.

The hospice offers treatment for all opportunistic infections of AIDS. It aims to provide *palliative* care, combining active and compassionate therapies to comfort and support individuals living with a life threatening illness. During periods of illness and bereavement, staff members strive to meet the physical, psychological, social and spiritual needs of the patients, while remaining sensitive to personal, cultural and religious values, beliefs and practices. Palliative care will start at the time of diagnosis and with combined holistic therapies, opportunistic illness is treated.

There is a unique spirit of teamwork among the doctors, nurses, counsellors, peer outreach workers and the strong contingent of volunteers. There is a sense of community here, as the families of the patients are given small tasks, and thereby integrated into the hospital schedule. HOPE's objectives here are to improve the health of the infected or affected children and mothers, to ensure the basic health and educational rights of the children, and finally to create a positive enabling environment within the community.

The administrator is Suvabrota Das. He has a background in community health care. He says that it is "very hard to combat the stigma and fear of AIDS". He admitted that even he, despite his background in health care, had to be trained that it was okay to touch a person with AIDS, adding, with a wry smile, that he had a sleepless night after his first time doing it.

Death is a sad fact of life at the hospice. As part of their palliative care, the dying patients are counselled before death, to ensure that their passing is peaceful. Their families come to visit from home as well to give comfort to them in their last days.

Target groups:

- HIV/AIDS infected children
- HIV/AIDS infected parents
- Post natal care of affected children below 18 months
- Affected children aged up to 12 years who have lost either both parents or the earning member among the parents due to HIV
- Pregnant HIV infected mothers.

Arunima AIDS hospice

Profile:

Munni, 18 years old, is from Howrah. She was diagnosed as HIV+ during pregnancy. Her baby, who is now 6 months old, will be tested for HIV at 18 months. She also had TB, but has now been treated for that. She is taking Septran DS, Anti Retro Viral Therapy. Her husband, Budha, also HIV+, is employed as a 'peer educator' on HIV.

The hospice offers the following services:

- A 10 bed in-patient care unit for children with primary-level emergency management and procedures
- Bi-weekly out-patient clinics
- Structured counselling services
- Elaborate nutritional care
- Weekly in-house psychiatric consultation
- Socio-legal support as and when necessary through networking with competent organisations
- Home based care (at a rudimentary stage)
- Rehabilitation support.

Suvabrota Das, hospice administrator

A group of Irish volunteers plan their improvements to the outdoor area

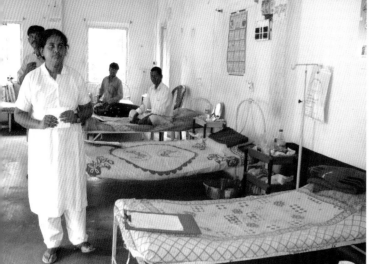

The nurse in the male ward

The outdoor area at the hospice

Plans for the Future:

Since HOPE's involvement in the work of this hospice is relatively recent, there is a constant ongoing effort to improve services even further:

- Providing holistic care and treatment for infected children and mothers in the well-equipped hospice
- The further development of home-based care, training the caregivers, family members and other community members involved
- Working on reducing the discrimination against those living with HIV/AIDS, and on promoting sustained clinical, psychological and social care and support for the children and their families

- Continuing to provide holistic support to the infected children in the form of nutrition, education and life skills training, to ensure their complete cognitive development
- Conducting training programmes for those who have contact with HIV/AIDS affected families
- Conducting awareness and sensitisation camps within the communities in which the children live
- Conducting stakeholder meetings within the community with local influential people and developing linkages with government hospitals and laboratories.

A little girl minds her baby brother at Arunima [Kate Cotter]

---

[1] Luce, 2006: 342. [2] Sen, 2000: 153. [3] Luce, 2006: 343. [4] www.UNICEF.org [5] Sen, 2000: 144. [6] Sen, 2000: 226.

education

2 **Education**
projects

Two little buddies in their HOPE uniforms head
home to Panditya Girl's Home for their lunch

PROJECT	PARTNER NGOs
1. Holistic Education Project	HKF, HIVE, SEED, SPAN, MJCC, PBKOJP, SICW, MBBCDS, ABWU, BPWT
2. Educational Sponsorship for Poor Children	SEED, SICW, ABWU, HKF, PBKOJP
3. Strengthening Institutional Care through Education	JPISC

"One test of the correctness of educational procedure is the happiness of the child"

Maria Montessori (1870-1952), Italian educator.

Spotlight 3: Illiteracy In India

One little boy from the HOPE Boy's Home reads from one of his textbooks

Rabindranath Tagore, the Bengali Nobel Prize winner, dreamt of an India "where the mind is without fear and the head is held high; where knowledge is free" and "where the mind is led forward into ever-widening thought and action".[1] The mind of his dreams is one that has been nurtured from an early age and given every opportunity to learn and develop. Sadly, this is usually not the case for the poor who live in India.

No matter where you live in the world, if you cannot confidently read a newspaper, look up a telephone book, fill in an official form, write a love letter or, now, send an email to another country, you will probably feel excluded, disempowered and out of step with the world around you. You may have managed to cope with your literacy problems by compensating for them in other ways, but it is still a nagging gap in one's social repertoire. It will also affect the range of possibilities one can expect in life, ruling out most gainful employment. It usually means being relegated to the ranks of the unemployed or at least the unskilled sectors of the labour force, whether one likes it or not. This can be deeply frustrating because of course it has no bearing on one's actual level of intelligence.

This is the lot of many, many millions of Indians. Of all Indian adults, only 66 per cent of them can read or write. We must remember India's postcolonial status, however, and note that the adult literacy rate in 1951, shortly after independence, was only 18 per cent. So achievements have been made, but not fast enough. After all, China, with its comparable population size, has an adult literacy rate of 90 per cent. Ironically, at the same time, India produces about a million engineering graduates every year. The continued funding of elite English-medium universities, especially the fifteen Indian Institutes of Technology (IITs) that produce some of the best scientific and engineering minds in the world, is, sadly, achieved at the expense of primary education for the masses.[2] Access to this type of technological education has been "essentially appropriated by upper caste, urban, high status families".[3]

Elitism percolates right down through the Indian education system. For example, it has become more prestigious for children to go to English medium schools like Loreto College in Kolkata. The effect of this elitism is that the Bengali or Hindi medium schools decline when they are not as much in demand. Those who go to these schools then often have to supplement their schooling with private tuition to compensate for poor standards. This unjust situation is of course a major disincentive for keeping children in school and may lead to their dropping out. Amartya Sen says, "effective elementary education has in practice ceased to be free in substantial parts of the country, which of course is a violation of a basic right".[4] Also, while in theory government schools are supposed to be free, anecdotal evidence suggests that some corrupt school administrators ask money from pupils that they should not have to pay.

Article 45 of the 1950 Indian Constitution decreed that there should be free and compulsory education for all children until the age of fourteen. In the early 1950s, 56 per cent of the education budget went to primary education. Pressure from the higher classes in Indian society led to more funding going to higher education that could benefit their own children.[5] The statistics that result from this class and caste bias are staggering, indeed damning. Half of all Indian children aged between six and eighteen do not go to school at all. Only 53 per cent of households have access to a primary school, and only 20 per cent of them to a secondary school. One in every forty primary schools in India operates either in the open air or in tents.[6] India has the worst pupil-teacher ratio in the world and the Indian illiterate population is more than the population of North America and Japan combined.[7]

Access to education is of course a basic human right, and every child should ideally be able to maximise her or his particular talents. The social benefits of literacy, especially for women, can never be overestimated, including "improvements in standards of hygiene, reduction in infant and child mortality rates, decline in population growth rates, increase in labour productivity, rise in civic consciousness, greater political empowerment and democratisation, and even an improved sense of national unity".[8] However, even if we approach this issue in purely instrumental terms, a high illiteracy rate makes no sense to the economy. The lack of what economists term human capital exerts a huge cost on Indian economic development. Basic literacy is a requirement for even the most rudimentary industrial job, never mind in information technology, which is such a strong pillar of the Indian economy at present. As Tharoor says, "illiteracy is a self-imposed handicap in a race we have no choice but to run".[9]

Even if children are initially enrolled in school, the dropout rate is often very high. It increases in classes 3 to 5, when it is reported to be at 50 per cent for boys and 58 per cent for girls.[10] It is important to express one's scepticism of such broad statistics because of the variations across such a vast and complex nation. However, in general, the dropout from school is caused by a variety of factors like these:

- Pressure to work to support their families – there is a close relationship between child illiteracy and child labour (see Spotlight 4). When families are poor, educating children, especially girls, is not a priority as they need income straight away to help them survive. Children are viewed as workers from a young age, especially if the parents themselves are uneducated. If choices have to be made between educating boys and girls, the boys will win out every time as they are seen to be a support system for the parent's old age. In rural areas, collecting water and firewood is seen as girl's work. Also, problems of illness and/or addiction within the families impinge upon the children. For example, if the fathers are alcoholics or drug addicts, girls will have to care for their younger siblings while their mothers are at work. If the mothers get sick, girls will have to do their mother's work so that she doesn't lose her job. Also, in the cities, many of the poor are seasonal migrants from rural areas, where they may have to return at harvest time.

- The high cost of private education – facilities and teaching standards are so poor in many schools that pupils and their parents have to pay for private tuition to compensate.

- An inappropriate and outdated curriculum – children may be uninterested in their studies, as they appear to be irrelevant to their lives.

- A poor learning environment at home, especially if they do not have electricity and there are many other young children that have to be cared for.

- The poor physical state of schools and the teaching the children receive - there is often a low level of parent satisfaction with schooling, and the lack of female teachers discourages parents from sending girls to school.

- Incentives like the midday meal are often not administered properly. In some places, water quality is poor, the cooks are not paid regularly and food goes missing.[11]

There is massive inequality in the Indian education system. One's chance of gaining access to elementary education varies dramatically depending upon which region one lives in, which class and which caste one is born into, and whether one is a boy or a girl. The variations throughout India are enormous. Adult literacy in Kerala stands at almost 100 per cent compared to 66 per cent in India overall and 44 per cent in the state of Bihar. Only about a third of Dalits are literate. There are only 71 literate women for every 100 literate men. Of Indians aged 15-24, 87 per cent of males can read and write, but only 77 per cent of females.[12] More than 50 per cent of girls fail to enrol in school, and those who do enrol are likely to drop out by the age of 12.[13] At this age, among India's poor, a girl is almost of marriageable age, and they see no point in keeping her in school. Kerala performs the best regarding female literacy, and Rajasthan and Bihar the worst. According to the 1991 Census, the enrolment of girls in schools was less than half that of boys in Utter Pradesh, Rajasthan and Bihar.[14] Overall, there is a steady trend of the gender gap closing in relation to literacy, but change is slow in general and non-existent in many regions.

Kolkata's own Professor Amartya Sen used some of his Nobel Prize money to set up the Pratichi Trust in 1999, whose goal was to assess and improve primary education in North East India and Bangladesh. His research team visited schools in selected regions of West Bengal, Jharkhand and Bangladesh. The first report was published in 2002 and the results were indeed depressing. The Trust found an extremely low standard of primary education in the region, with teacher absenteeism posing a particular problem. This was much worse in schools where the majority of the pupils came from Scheduled Caste and Scheduled Tribe families, i.e. from the poorest members of the communities. He reported then that the teachers' unions had tried to defend their members from censure and discipline, exacerbating this unjust situation. In his opinion, this had been further worsened by the increasing class barrier between teachers and pupils, following pay rises for teachers. Despite having defended pay rises for teachers in the past, he now sees these as part of the problem rather than the solution.[15]

The Pratichi Trust's second report, launched in December 2009, found some improvements in school attendance and pupils' performance, teacher absenteeism was not as bad and parent satisfaction was higher. This, no doubt, was due in no small part to the activities of the Trust themselves, who had been engaging regularly with teachers' unions over the years. Some serious problems continue to exist however. Firstly, the school inspection system is in great need of improvement. Secondly, the provision of the midday meal needs to be extended to every child. While this is improving, more needs to be done as it has been found to be a major incentive for parents to send their children to school. We must remember that in these areas, hunger is part of life for many. In West Bengal, it is estimated that 16.5 per cent of the rural population

A HOPE coaching centre

barely manages to have one meal a day, with another 3.5 per cent not able to do even that. The Trust has urged the state government to increase the funding it gives to Integrated Child Development Services (ICDS) and thus improving the provision of the midday meal.[16] Thirdly, there seems to be a great need for curricular reform. The content seems to be very difficult for small children, and this leads parents to seek out costly private tuition for them that they can ill-afford.[17] This can only lead to a downward spiral where children drop out of school prematurely and join the swelling ranks of uneducated child labourers.

Lack of education and ignorance keeps the unequal and unjust status quo intact. It keeps the poor from engaging with public life in a constructive fashion and adds fuel to the fires of social and ethnic divisions. Their grievances are more likely to be expressed violently because their ability to develop and express an informed opinion is hampered severely by illiteracy. Continued exclusion from proper primary, secondary and tertiary education ensures the widening and deepening of the severe oppression suffered by India's poor.

The aims of HOPE's education programme are:

- **To create awareness among the poor of the need to educate their children**
- **To facilitate processes of education for poor children by supporting them**
- **To encourage the parent community, the community leaders, the child employers, the political system and the bureaucracy towards taking children out of work and enrolling them in school.**

Education is a crucial instrument for bringing about social, economic and political transformation, and is at the heart of the work of the Hope Foundation. Equity and social justice are enshrined in the Indian Constitution, and can only be realised through quality education for all children. Since education is a fundamental right of every child born in India, the onus is on the state to provide education customised to the real needs of society, especially geared towards the marginalized groups who have been left behind by the architects of the rapid economic growth of the past decade. Sadly, it often falls on NGOs to provide the education that should be provided by the state. The HOPE education programme aims to ensure the educational rights of the poor children in Kolkata. It emphasises providing education, nutrition and overall health for the vulnerable children of impoverished families, encouraging street children into education and addressing adolescent issues. This work is done in partnership with other NGOs in the city, as well as by HOPE itself.

1 Holistic Education Project

Sobha teaches at the crèche in Kasba Girl's Home

This project aims to improve the educational level of poor children, ensuring their basic educational rights. It has several interconnected aspects, as outlined below:

Pre-Primary Education and Coaching Support for Underprivileged Children:

HOPE, along with its local partner NGOs, aims to ensure basic educational rights for Kolkata's poor slum-dwelling children.

HOPE runs **pre-school education centres** for the children under the age of six. This allows their mothers and fathers to work and earn more money for their families. The children at the crèches receive:

- Nutritious food
- Health checkups
- Mainstreaming
- Educational support

HOPE also runs educational guidance centres, called 'coaching centres', for first-generation learners who already attend formal schools. In these coaching centres qualified teachers guide the children, ensuring an improvement in school performance and thereby increasing the probability that the children will stay in school. The children's parents are usually uneducated and possibly illiterate. The

This HOPE coaching centre operates inside a metal container. Imagine the heat in here when it is 40 degrees outside, and yet they all concentrate hard on their lessons

HOPE COACHING CENTRE, CHETLA SLUM. This coaching centre exists for seven years, currently helping 95 children. They have to take classes in shif because there is no room. [Kelly Campbell]

living conditions they endure are cramped, they have very poor services, so they are not conducive to study. Also, they will be put to work if they are not in school, so every hour they spend in the coaching centres protects them from child labour and other forms of abuse.

In the coaching centres the children receive:

- Nutritious food
- Health checkups
- Mainstreaming into formal education
- Educational support
- School uniforms
- Educational materials
- Counselling support

Over the years, HOPE's coaching support has helped many thousands of children to gain admittance to schools and to continue their formal education. The more demand there is for government educational services, the more onus is upon them to improve the provision and delivery of these services. With the support of HOPE, local NGOs have succeeded in reducing the incidence of children dropping out of school early. It is also important to include the mothers of these children in the overall programme. Opportunities are created for them to become economically active, and hence more independent.

All of the children that HOPE take care of are provided with both group and individual counselling if they need it, and all the children take part in fun recreational activities. These are vital for any child's healthy psychological development. They celebrate the myriad of festivals that dot the Indian calendar. Key community figures often join in the fun, as a further motivation for everyone to get involved.

> **It costs about €6,000 to run a coaching centre for a year, with an average of 50 children.**
> **This pays for the teacher, food, books, schoolbag, health and psychological support.**
> **HOPE funds 45 of these centres.**

The crèche at Panditya Girl's Home

The following are some of the several partner NGOs that work with HOPE on the Holistic Education Project:

HOPE PARTNER: MAYURBHANJ JOINT CITIZEN CENTRE (MJCC)

MISSION STATEMENT:
MJCC is committed to provide sustainable development for the underprivileged and vulnerable children living in difficult circumstances with the provision of education, vocational training, health awareness and services, nutrition, counselling, recreation, awareness of rights and capacity building to reach that goal.

Mr. Yusef, Director of MJCC

HOPE has funded MJCC education and healthcare programmes since 2004. The initial funding proposal to HOPE was to keep girls in school until Class 10, to the age of about 14. They are also involved in Childwatch, having created education centres for street children who work as beggars. Government schools often reject these children because of their illegal status. As well as receiving funding from HOPE, they also get some funds from Save the Children UK, CINI-ASHA and the Governments of India and of West Bengal.

MJCC was founded in the early 1990s. The main thrust of their work is to organise urban and rural communities of the poor to enhance their condition through self-help. It emphasises three basic principles – participation, development and enabling.

Mr. Yusef, its Director, was a founder member. He came from a very poor background himself and got into social work because he didn't want others to suffer like he had himself. After five years of voluntary work, he got support from UNICEF and Save the Children UK to set up an NGO. He is a very committed person, and takes pride in individual cases where he has helped people.

He operates in the port area of Kolkata, where there is huge poverty and unemployment. There is no government support for those who live in illegal slums like this. There is a very high birth rate here and strong discrimination against girls is the norm. They drop out of school in class 5 or 6, at the age of 9 or 10, and parents do not want to send them to school after that. A lot of girls are married at 14 and will have their first baby at 15. Parental responsibility stops when the girl is married. However, they try to counsel parents and intervene to stop these child marriages.

Some of their many activities, many of which are funded by HOPE, include:
- Health awareness programmes, for example on HIV and on breastfeeding
- Training of Community Health Volunteers and social worker home visits
- Eighteen schools for classes 1-4 in Khidderpore
- A programme for trafficked children
- A remedial coaching centre
- 26 self-help groups for the empowerment of women
- A mobile medical unit running primary healthcare clinics
- Youth clubs
- Vocational training
- A childwatch programme
- A birth registration programme

Educating girls is the key to solving so many social problems

Coaching centre run by MJCC at Khidderpore. The primary healthcare clinic is visible in the background, operating at the same time

HOPE PARTNER: SEED

MISSION:

To work collaboratively to uplift vulnerable children, to co-ordinate a network for the distribution of information and to share with others. Representing the voice of many, we speak as one for the rights of children wherever they may be.

Vision:

SEED believes in action as a force for change: to protect children at risk, to protect their human rights and to prevent future generations from suffering the same lack of choices that forces children on to the street at present. They believe that it is possible to achieve better lives for vulnerable children, and the way to do this is through the children themselves. SEED has a dream of seeing children shaping their own lives in the manner of their own choosing.

SEED provides help and shelter to children in need in Kolkata's tough urban environment. It has six shelter homes for boys and girls. HOPE funds one of these girl's homes. HOPE also funds SEED in its work in helping 600 children in four coaching centres and a crèche.

Observation notes:

SEED Coaching Centres

The co-ordinator of this project is Salil Dhara. He has a Diploma in Pharmacy and Ophthalmology, but decided to switch into social work and do an MSW. He is a dedicated, honourable and intelligent young man, a true expert on the urban landscape in which he works.

Perfect Hill Dump:

Words fail to express the horrors of the municipal dump. It is so enormous that there are roads over it that can be driven upon like mountain roads. The rag pickers, those who slave here for a few rupees, have to compete with rats, dogs and wild pigs. The air is putrid from the rotting rubbish and there is permanent dust and smoke. It is not fit for animals here, never mind for human beings. Once you have seen this place, you have seen Hell.

The government has no recycling programme, as the rag pickers do their work for them. They save money for the municipality because they don't have to employ workers to empty the trucks at the dump. Rag pickers are paid Rs. 12/kg for plastics, Rs. 2/kg for rubber sandal soles, Rs. 10/kg for iron and Rs. 10 for a big bag of fruit seeds. So private business profits from the labours of these poor women and children. The problem is that after the age of 13

The ironically named Perfect Hill Dump. That people have to try to eke out a living here is an enormous injustice

or 14, children need to work to survive, so there is what Salil terms a 'demotivating factor' to stay under the care of the community projects.

The education project here has no property of its own, but they pay a private school Rs. 1000 a month to use theirs. They need new premises. They cater to 150 children here, with six full time teachers.

Howrah

The building used by SEED is a former hospital for employees of Howrah station. It is a heaving wreck with no electricity, but they make the best of their situation. They use a small generator during the day, but they cannot afford to run it at night.

The children here are aged from six to fourteen. Most of them are migrants from Bihar and Utter Pradesh. Many of the older ones are 'cement children'. This is one of the worst forms of child labour, where little boys' bodies are twisted and distorted from carrying huge bags of cement for sale. It is hard

SEED Crèche, Howrah

Salil Dhara, co-ordinator of SEED holistic education project

SEED Coaching centre, Shalimar Yard

to get these 'cement children' to go to coaching centres. They are 13 or 14 and it is normal to work at that age. It is hard to motivate them, as the Rs. 50 a day they earn is a significant contribution to their households.

It is hoped that education will save the smaller ones from the same fate. Their guardians are mostly grandparents, or single parents where the man has deserted or the woman has died. They pay a token sum of Rs. 10 a month to have their children attend the coaching centre or Rs. 20 a month for the crèche. These kids have no official identity, as their parents have no voter ID or Resident Card and the children were not registered at birth. This restricts their opportunities in the future for education and work. The parents or guardians need income-generating projects. Five of the mothers are employed by the project to maker breakfast and dinner (tiffin) for the children in a community kitchen. They are paid Rs. 1000 a month, making a huge difference to their family income.

Shalimar Yard 1 and 2

These centres exist for a few years – they save these children from even more hardship and various kinds of child labour. It improves the drop out rate from school to keep them in the coaching centres for as long as possible. These children lead such hard lives and these little coaching centres, while very basic, are nevertheless civilised oases of calm and of learning in the middle of their otherwise harsh and chaotic environments.

This 12-year-old girl had to leave school to work to pay for medicine for her sick mother. She works as a housemaid washing dishes in the mornings. The coaching centre is a lifeline for her, her only connection with learning. She earns Rs. 700 a month

These two brothers and one sister are aged 12, 11 and 8. The boy on the left has polio. The middle child, Pramod, and his mother get up at 4am to make bread, then go to the railway station at 6am to sell it. Then he goes to school for 2–3 hours in the morning. He then starts at 4pm in the coaching centre until 7pm and goes to bed at 9pm. His mother works as a maid in the mornings. He has his midday meal at school.

Mission:

SPAN is guided by the mission to conduct an extensive, intensive and participatory sustainable development process through people's empowerment.

Vision:

SPAN envisages an Indian society that is democratic, economically productive and equitable, socially just and environmentally sound. They wish to create an enabling situation where marginalized and disadvantaged people will have their opinion expressed through making informed choices on any national or state policies that will affect their lives. Since 1989, they have been running health and education programmes for the urban poor, focussing especially on the needs of destitute women and children. Since 2001, they also have worked on a campaign against child labour.

Creche run by SPAN in Chitpur. This is Partha, the co-ordinator of the holistic education project

The teachers at the Chitpur crèche

Children recite a poem at the Chitpur crèche

Observation notes:

Chitpur Colony

This is a holistic education project in the middle of an unauthorised slum. Partha, a SPAN social worker, told me that there are 3,500 slums in Kolkata and half of them are unauthorised. This means that they can be torn down and demolished at any time by the municipality. All the inhabitants of this slum are Muslim migrants from Bangladesh and rural areas of West Bengal, especially the Sundarbans area to the south.

Coaching centre run by SPAN in a government school at Marcus Square in the city centre

This slum is in the North Port area and HOPE funds three projects there. SPAN also gets funding from Action Aid and other agencies. They work in both urban and rural West Bengal.

SPAN advises people of their entitlements and tries to empower them to seek government services. In that way, they bridge the gap between the people and the state. They run a coaching centre, which children can attend after they come home from government schools. They go to school from 6-11am, and then come here at 11.30am. They help them with their homework and they protect them from parental pressure to work. They operate the crèche from 8-11am in the same room. They work with 90 boys and girls here in total. HOPE funds uniforms, books, schoolbags and food for them, and social workers do home visits to encourage children to come here.

Marcus Square, city centre:

This is an Integrated Child Development Scheme (ICDS) project. The government's social welfare dept is supposed to provide one for every 1,000 children under five in the cities and every 1,500 in rural areas. SPAN runs this coaching centre at a government school, given to them free by the municipality. Normal government schools run from 6-10am, then the coaching centre runs from 11-5pm. They teach 65 children, with an average of about 20 in a class. SPAN set it up as a backup to the government system, making sure the children are kept safe and focussed on study. It is a holistic project, in that they address the child's entire set of needs. For example, SPAN makes sure that the school provides the midday meal that it is required to by law. They want to ensure "access not just to education, but to quality education".

Teachers at SPAN Coaching centre at Marcus Square

They also try to empower the poor to seek their entitlements in health and education. They have groups for youths and for mothers, empowering and involving everyone. Protecting children's rights is very important to them. Many children don't make it to school, as they grow too old, so they try to give them informal education, under the Childwatch programme. They try to involve the whole community in the development process, through the medium of focus groups.

All Bengal Women's Union was founded in 1932. The founding women were from influential families, like wives of magistrates and other social luminaries. It developed because of the proliferation of prostitution at this time in Calcutta. Between the two world wars, the number of sailors and soldiers had increased considerably in Calcutta and the 'flesh trade' was buoyant. A small number of girls were rescued from brothels and given refuge. The Great Bengal Famine of 1943 saw a huge influx of destitute people from the countryside, and as a result the home housed 50 girls and women by 1945. It expanded steadily over the years, and is currently a large organisation that takes care of hundreds of girls and women.

Currently they employ about 200 staff in their enormous property on Eliot Road in Kolkata city centre. They have four residential shelter homes. There are 200 in their children's home, 50 in their home for young adults, 25 in their home for trafficked girls, 6-10 in their midway home, as well as 25 in their old age home. There are 250 children in their primary school, 100 more in their crèche, and they have a 'bridging class' for children brought in during the school year and in need of special help. They also have an outreach programme for about 2,000 children in West Bengal.

They receive most of their funding from the government. They had been receiving funding from Save the Children UK, but in recent years they withdrew funding, as they moved on to war zones and more needy areas. They were therefore very grateful when HOPE moved in with their funding in 1999, so that they could continue with their work.

HOPE has funded a coaching centre and a crèche at **All Bengal Women's Union** since 1999. These children have been provided with supplementary nutrition on a regular basis to help them cope with malnutrition. Hence, most of the children under the project enjoy good health. In the short-term, regular food has motivated the children to enrol and attend coaching centres regularly.

Awareness Generation:

This aspect of HOPE's work aims to generate an enabling child-friendly environment within the community, so that the children can continue their education in schools. Throughout last year the project has organised 100 awareness and sensitisation camps or campaigns in different pockets of Kolkata and Howrah. HOPE, with the help of grass-root organisations, has been able to generate awareness among several thousands of people living in the slums and streets of Kolkata and Howrah. The issues include:

* The basic rights of children
* The concept of child protection
* The need for and benefits of education
* The basic health needs of children
* The basic psychological needs of children
* The procedures involved in school admission.

Capacity-building for schoolteachers:

Research has shown that formal schoolteachers are often unaware of child protection issues and children's rights. It has been found that this lack of knowledge can contribute to dropout problems in formal schools. HOPE has designed a training module for these teachers, to help improve their

Outdoor classes at the school in Birbhum, rural West Bengal

abilities to teach, motivate and discipline in a constructive fashion. This approach encourages child-friendly education, creating a positive learning environment that ensures physical safety, emotional security and psychological well being for every child.

Advocacy and stakeholder meetings:

HOPE and its partners raise awareness about its educational work and children's rights through networking and advocacy among various stakeholders. This occurs among both governmental and non-governmental groups and individuals. As a result of these group meetings, awareness camps and the numerous official visits, the broader community is becoming more aware of the dehumanising conditions endured by these vulnerable children and their families.

Educational Support for Children with Special Needs:

The Society for Indian Children's Welfare (SICW) has 25 years experience in running an educational centre and residential unit for children with special needs. It has been in partnership with the Hope Foundation since 2005.

Educational Support for Tribal Children:

Mohammad Bazar Backward Classes Development Society (MBBCDS), a partner since 2006, provides education to the poor marginalised tribal children of Birbhum district, an area in West Bengal that is predominantly inhabited by the Santhal tribe. This group are living in some of the worst socio-economic conditions in India, as they have been neglected, oppressed and exploited. The tribe as a whole suffers from illiteracy, poverty, exploitation, lack of access to government services and other social injustices. MBBCDS makes sure that the local community is integrated directly in their development work, which provides pre-primary education to thirty children under five and supplementary coaching support to seventy children who are in formal school.

Observation notes:

SICW

The SICW centre is dedicated to working with twelve children between two and seven years who have special needs due to cerebral palsy. It aims to make the children as self reliant as possible and offer them a quality standard of living. As these children are dependant on caregivers for everything, they are taught daily living skills, including toilet training, feeding themselves if possible, bathing, changing, indicating needs, following instructions, how to become more aware of their surroundings, and connecting with peers and adults around them. As these children require help with activities of daily living, all opportunities throughout the day are seen as a learning process. Children are taught with picture books and posters. It has been found that the intense educational and speech stimulation process for these children is influencing the children in a positive way. Physiotherapy forms an integral part of their rehabilitation to improve their motor skills.

Almost all of the children are orphans. Some are 'relinquished children' of single parents. They have contacts in hospitals and police stations who arrange for children to be sent to them. There is an age limit of six years, but some are kept on after that age if they have nowhere else to go. The children get excellent care here. Special chairs are made from timber for each child to fit their size. The staff here are very dedicated to the children. The co-ordinator is Ronita Bhattacharyya (B.Ed. in Special Ed.). The Special Needs Supervisor, Sarita Dhir, has worked voluntarily for seven years. She initiated contact with Maureen and drew up the proposal for funding from HOPE.

Ronita, Special Needs Supervisor at SICW

Another aspect of their work is that they arrange foreign adoptions for the children. The staff use a very touching term for these while preparing the children for their adoptions - their 'forever families'. SICW and the Missionaries of Charity, founded by Mother Teresa, are the only two NGOs permitted to have children adopted abroad from West Bengal. One little girl showed me a wallet of photos of the couple in Poland who are in the process of adopting her. She points to the man in the photo and repeats "Daddy, Daddy". The adoption process is a long and protracted one.

Left: This child, Fatima, was rescued from the street, having been chained to a railing by her parents for the purposes of begging.
Centre: Notice board displaying the children's adoptive families. Right: Irish volunteers Mary and Kate with the children at SICW.

2 Educational Sponsorship Project

This aspect of HOPE's work provides support for destitute marginalized children, who cannot afford to continue their education. Improving the educational status of this marginalized poor sector of society will help to bring about positive social change. Through this project, HKF, SICW, SEED, PBKOJP and ABWU supports these underprivileged children, especially girls, to continue their secondary and higher secondary level education, and if needed, higher levels of education as well.

Gora, Geeta and Maureen with the new bus

HOPE firmly believes that educational services provided by NGOs should complement existing government services and seek ways to improve them, rather than duplicate services that already exist. The project tries to develop a process of education and attainments that ensure the children's ability to acquire knowledge, communicate, and participate in community life. It alters an individual's and a community's collective perceptions, aspirations and goals as well as improving the ability and means to attain them.

From past experience, HOPE believes that education cannot be viewed in isolation. Rather a student's educational performance is very closely linked with her/his nutritional and psychological status. These children mostly start out malnourished, leading to their underperformance in school. HOPE also helps the children to improve their physical and psychological health in order to maximise their educational performance.

HOPE runs an education sponsorship programme providing nutrition, educational materials including uniforms, pencils, books etc. The cost of becoming a sponsor is approximately €250 per year. Many children who have been supported through this programme are now entering the professional world themselves and returning to offer as much support to HOPE and partners as possible.

The arrival of the new school bus in Dec. 2009 is a very big event! The new bus will make life much easier for the girls

3 Strengthening Institutional Care Through Education

The challenge of children who are in conflict with the law and children in need of care and protection has been the subject of constant and widespread public discussion in recent years. Whenever the problem assumed alarming proportions, the government exercised its power to contain the problem through institutionalising the offenders. Unfortunately, few systematic, co-ordinated and planned efforts have been implemented to understand their problem behaviour and its varied consequences, or to evolve appropriate strategies and institutional arrangements to meet these challenges.

HOPE, with its local partner JPISC, has implemented programmes of a multi-dimensional nature, both in urban and rural settings, to initiate and pursue action-oriented changes in the micro societies. The Institute seeks to remedy poverty-related problems through capacity-building initiatives. The homes provide care and support to child victims of various forms of social oppression and facilitate social reintegration. The counselling component of the project aims to reduce a child's distress and discomfort and help her/him to recuperate physically and emotionally. About 200 children have been provided with coaching and remedial support in developing and sustaining an interest in their studies.

Having experienced running the education project in three government-run homes, HOPE noted that the personnel of these homes often lacked knowledge on counselling, guidance and the methods of treatment for children who have been subjected to various forms of trauma. In order to achieve its goal of improving the treatment and rehabilitation of the children, JPISC is providing skills development training to about 120 staff from the homes. The targeted participants are superintendents, social workers, teachers, and counsellors, as well as all other staff involved in giving care and support to the children. All three government-run homes are being targeted.

The objectives of this training are to sensitise and orient staff on the rights-based approach to child development and the basic tenets of the Juvenile Justice (Care and Protection of Children) Act 2000; to clarify the roles and responsibilities of different personnel involved in managing the homes; to enhance their knowledge of both the theory and practice of managing children's behavioural problems, and to encourage the adoption of an integrated approach towards the social reintegration of the children.

[1] Tharoor, 2007a: 164.
[2] Luce, 2006: 52.
[3] Raju, 2006: 85.
[4] Sen, 2005: 217.
[5] Varma, 2006: 104.
[6] 7th All India Education Survey, 2002
[7] Tharoor, 2007a:161.
[8] Tharoor, 2007a: 163.
[9] Tharoor, 2007a: 164.
[10] 7th All India Education Survey, 2002
[11] Bose, 2006: 161.
[12] UNICEF Statistics - India, 2009.
[13] 7th All India Education Survey, 2002
[14] Bose, 2006: 159.
[15] Sen, 2005: 216-218.
[16] Roy, 2009.
[i17] Sen, 2009.

child Protection

8 Child Protection
projects

PROJECT	PARTNER NGOs
1. Child Watch Project	HKF, HIVE, ABWU, SPAN, MJCC, PBKOJP, BPWT
2. Protection Homes for Boys and Girls	HKF, SEED, PBKOJP, BPWT, HRLN, ABWU
3. Anti-trafficking Project	HCWS

Spotlight 4: Child Labour in India

The Campaign Against Child Labour (CACL) defines child labour as:

"Children prematurely leading adult lives, working with or without wages, under conditions damaging to their physical, social, emotional and spiritual development, denying them their basic rights to education, health and development. This includes children working in any sector, occupation or process, including the formal and non-formal, organised and unorganised, within or outside the family". [1]

Using this definition, child labour is an immense problem in India, with many millions of children being horribly exploited every day. India is home to the largest child labour force in the world, amounting to a quarter of all the world's child labourers. [2] The problem is difficult to enumerate exactly, as many children are never officially registered at birth. On paper, they do not exist. Official Indian statistics claim that there are 12.59 million child labourers, but UNICEF, on the other hand, puts the number at more than twice that, at 35 million. A higher estimate is a staggering 40 million, which corresponds to the number of children 'missing' from school. [3] UNICEF also estimates that 12 per cent of children aged 5-14 are engaged in child labour. That is a staggering one in every eight children.

Child labour is or course illegal under the 1950 Constitution, which was in fact very progressive for its time. However, the labour legislation is woefully out of date. All of the relevant Acts only define under 14s as children, instead of under 18s, as dictated by the United Nations Convention on the Rights of the Child (UNCRC) in 1989. The rate of conviction under child labour laws is very poor, as laws are not properly enforced.

In order to understand this, we firstly need to make a distinction between child *work* and child *labour*. The big difference between the two is whether the child gets a chance to go to school and get an education. Sometimes a child may go to work after school to supplement the family income. While this is not of course ideal, it may be the best one can hope for, providing a form of work-based training in a harsh social environment. At least they are still exposed to learning, expanding their minds and potentially opening up future opportunities. However, when a child is forced to work *instead* of attending school, it leads to the blatant abuse of children's human rights. They spend their days working in dirty and hazardous workplaces, performing mind-numbing tasks that impede their development instead of enjoying mind-expanding classes at school.

Streets, houses, shops and rubbish piles are still filled with children who have been forced into labour. Most children work because they have no choice, being forced into it by parents who are poor and unemployed themselves. Most working children live in rural areas, and their work is in the agricultural sector and the domestic sector. Girls are subjected to even more exploitation, firstly because of gender stereotyping which suggests they are more suited to child minding and domestic labour and secondly because of sexual abuse. This makes their exploitation all the more invisible as much of it occurs within the family.

The context for this child labour in rural India is often that of bonded labour. This is very common in India, Pakistan and Bangladesh and usually involves the whole family. This occurs when a person's labour is demanded in return for a loan that is never paid off. The person is then tricked into working for little or no pay. In many cases, the loan is passed down from parent to child. Poor and bonded families also often 'sell' their children to contractors who promise lucrative jobs in the cities. The children end up working in hotels, brothels and in private homes. Bonded labourers are usually unable to defend themselves from abuse and they are bound by a displaced sense of duty to repay the debt owed by their family. They are caught in a trap from which they cannot escape. These families, and especially children, are actually slaves in the modern world.

Due to the illegal and clandestine nature of child labour, it is a hidden scourge that is very difficult to research. However, Human Rights Watch have published two major reports on bonded child labourers. They estimate the extent of this beleaguered group at somewhere between 60 and 115 million, and the majority are Dalits, the so-called 'untouchables' who continue to suffer intolerable discrimination and harassment. Bonded child labourers were found in seven industries: beedi (cigarette) making, silver, synthetic gemstones, silk, leather, agriculture and hand woven wool carpets. Their 2003 report focussed on the silk industry in particular. They describe the conditions:

"In the factories and workshops that make silk thread, children suffer injuries from the machines and from sharp threads. Sericin vapours from the boiling cocoons, smoke, diesel fumes from the machines, and poor ventilation cause respiratory ailments such as chronic bronchitis and asthma. From immersion in scalding water and handling dead worms, reelers' hands become raw, blistered, and sometimes infected. … Anesha K., eleven years old, started working when she was nine… She showed us lumpy scars on her hands and explained: "I didn't like working because my hands would get infected. I got holes in my hands because I put them in the hot water and then they got infected. I couldn't eat. I had to eat with a spoon". Anesha K.'s shins, ankles, and feet were covered with burn scars from boiling water".[4]

Child labour has been justified or minimised in various ways. It is often the case that parents want to start their children in the family's trade early, like in tea picking or carpet making, in order to keep the jobs within the family later. The thinking is that this is the best possible option that can be presented to the child. The government even went as far as calling many forms of child labour "a standard process of socialization" in 2001.[5] Employers sometimes claim that employing children is a form of welfare, as they feel sorry for their impoverished parents. Also, their so-called 'nimble fingers' make them attractive for employment making carpets and on cotton and vanilla plantations.[6]

Even some Gandhian activists approve of the reproduction of the family trade, because it is keeping traditional skills alive and offers children practical skills that they would not get in formal education.[7] This highly socially conservative approach, while well meaning in its own way, accepts the current status quo without questioning it. Surely in the twenty-first century, our goal should be to offer every child the *choice* to work at anything they wish, rather than being pushed into early child labour for the sake of keeping the class and caste system intact. The Indian state is reluctant to admit the existence and extent of this modern form of slavery. It is a dirty secret that does not tally with the image of the new Shining India.

India is home to many millions of children who have been denied all basic human rights. They live in hopeless poverty without access to education, medical support and treatment, shelter or even food. They grow up uncared for and are condemned to miserable conditions. Child slavery is rampant, violence against children endemic and the right to education, though now established by law, exists only on paper. Due to the blinkered form of development adopted by the Indian state and the resulting rampant urbanisation, the number of hungry, sick and exploited street and working children is growing rapidly. These are vulnerable children whose only home is on the streets, so their protection, nourishment, or even survival cannot be guaranteed.

In Kolkata, it is estimated that a staggering 250,000 children are forced to exist on the streets. These are *street children* in the fullest sense - children whose only shelter, if any, may be plastic sheeting or tiny shacks. Their circumstances vary. Some of them have migrated to the city from rural areas, alone or with their families, while others were born on the streets and grew up in the city's open public places. Not all of them are necessarily homeless or orphans, but come from families where there is no protection or direction from responsible adults. Many children run away from abusive and exploitative situations at home to live their lives alone on the streets of already overcrowded cities like Kolkata. Others are with their whole families who are trying to escape lives of destitution.

Protecting street children from violence, exploitation and abuse is an integral component of ensuring their rights to survival, growth and development. HOPE, whose projects spread across Kolkata and neighbouring Howrah, are working with the problems faced by these children such as child trafficking, child labour, sexual abuse, prostitution, solvent abuse and forced marriages, to mention but a few.

Through HOPE's Child Protection projects they aim to protect children from physical, emotional and sexual abuse as well as neglect. They help children grow up into confident, healthy and happy adults. In co-operation with its partners, the Hope Foundation runs nine protection homes for children who are orphaned, abandoned, HIV infected or affected, victims of trafficking or have special needs. In these homes, the children receive protection, nutrition, education, healthcare, rehabilitation, counselling, recreation, support and love.

Children enjoying art class

This project is an integrated programme that targets children who are at high risk from criminal and violent acts such as assault, physical abuse, sexual abuse and domestic violence.

Aims of Child Watch:

- To ensure a secure future, improved quality of life and basic rights for needy, vulnerable children who are at risk through the provision of holistic care on a 24-hour basis

- To eliminate child labour, protect children from different kinds of abuse, rehabilitate addicted children and ensure all children's rights of basic education and health

- Advocacy - networking with government or non-government organisations and awareness generation in the greater community.

This project offers:

- The provision of holistic care on a 24 hour basis
- Treatment and nutrition supplementation for severely malnourished children
- Mainstreaming of child labourers into school
- Detoxification, rehabilitation and accommodation of children who have been involved in substance abuse
- Life skill training for children
- Providing non-formal training for non school-goers who have passed school-going age
- Counselling
- Networking and lobbying with governments and other stakeholders on issues around child labour
- Organising camps and campaigns on child labour and child protection.

Nabadisha Project

HOPE's target group is the street children of Kolkata and Howrah, who have been deprived of their basic human rights. Some are lost or abandoned, while others have run away from lives of destitution and/or violence. These children are fending for themselves alone or in groups in extremely harsh environments. Others live with their families, but in equally severe conditions. Many children are suffering from various diseases including HIV/Aids. They are vulnerable to alcohol and drug abuse due to the extremity of their lives. Many have lived a life of violence and have been victims of physical, sexual and mental abuse and exploitation.

Working with its partners, the police, hospitals and the community, HOPE identifies the children who are "high risk" and protects them by providing medical assistance, counselling, education and recreational facilities. It is a sad fact that many thousands of vulnerable children are beyond HOPE's reach. However, through its advocacy and campaigning work, HOPE aims to change the official and public mindset, reinforcing that this level of poverty is unacceptable in the 21st century.

Educational Intervention:

HOPE provides education to street-involved children, child labourers and slum children on a daily basis. For this purpose, 30 drop-in centres have been established in areas where street children congregate. Each such centre caters for approximately 50 children. These centres are safe environments for children while they make the transition to become regular school-goers. As these children often have had no form of education or regulation in their lives, the teaching style is

Children enjoying art class

necessarily informal in these centres, thereby encouraging the children to stay and to progress with their education.

One example of this type of intervention is the unique Nabadisha Education Programme for street children. The Nabadisha (meaning 'New Directions') Programme has been working in synergy with the Kolkata police since August 2004. This group would not always be seen as a natural ally by street dwellers, but this project is a shining example for Indian police to emulate everywhere.

It operates in their stations in four areas of the city: Tollygunge, Gariahat, Topsia and New Market. The Hope Foundation Child Watch Project thereby holds classes and other activities for several hundred children who have been denied access to formal schooling. It is a holistic project, because it works on their education, their health, family life, counselling, receation and cultural activities.

Children at art class

Once a child comes through the door, every effort is made to meet all of her/his needs. Everything from immunisation camps to theatre workshops are part and parcel of the Nabadisha project. The mothers are also involved, as literacy, nutrition, health and hygiene classes are made available for them. This is very empowering for the women themselves and it also makes it more likely that they will want their children to stay on in education rather than becoming child labourers.

Many of these slum-dwelling children have originated in far-flung regions of India like Gujarat and Bihar. The harsh environment in Kolkata is therefore perhaps new to many of them. The children appreciate the centres so much. In their art classes, they draw, colour, and play with Lego with such intensity that it is as if their lives depend on it. Nothing else like this exists for them otherwise. It gives them some respite from their hard lives, and a chance to *be children*, if only for a few hours. It is also a gateway to a better, healthier and more fulfilled life.

Economic Intervention:

The high levels of tenacity of the hardcore street children has been used to their advantage when designing their rehabilitation programmes in the Child Watch Project. These programmes incorporate skills, which will enable them to be admitted for training in similar professions in the future. Participating in these vocational training programmes and finding work afterwards where they can excel helps the children to find some meaning and purpose in life.

Pinky, the teacher works with the children

Health Intervention:

The health education programme is an important aspect of the Child Watch Project. Serious medical problems can be prevented by the education the children receive in hygiene and grooming for everyday living. The benefits of this training can now be seen, as the children with whom HOPE work are well disciplined and well educated. The children are trained in basic hygiene, thereby keeping their bodies clean and safe. As well as this training, medicines are provided for day-to-day ailments. This is a positive step towards the improvement of the children's socio-economic and hygienic conditions. This programme has received much praise from the community. The organisation is well known and respected at a number of nursing homes and private hospitals in and around Howrah. Agreements have been made with these institutions to ensure that reduced rates are charged for children admitted from the health clinic referrals. These costs are paid by the health clinic.

Protective Intervention:

The Emergency Response Unit was initiated to provide palliative care to street people in order to bring some dignity to their lives at their ultimate time of need. The service reaches out to people who face emergencies on the streets of the city, prioritising especially Kolkata's many thousands of underprivileged children.

Through the night round programme, starving street children have been given food, clothing and temporary shelter at night. Sick and injured children have been hospitalised. High-risk girls have been placed in homes or night shelters. In each case, the program carefully assesses the capability of each family to protect and take care of the child. The child's wishes are also taken into account. If the assessment results in a positive outcome, counselling is provided to both the child and family and they are ultimately reunited. The night round programme has had a great impact on the number of children rescued and rehabilitated.

Counselling:

By using techniques such as problem solving, relaxation training, story-telling, self-monitoring and demonstration, children have been educated on subjects such as reproduction and sexual abuse, which may otherwise be difficult to talk about. In order to guard themselves against the dangers of the streets, children develop a protective shell and they may have become defensive and reticent. It is therefore necessary to ensure that the child is allowed enough time to talk so that their problems can be addressed seriously. There is a massive need for counselling for many of these children. Their psychological health is monitored as closely as their physical health by the HOPE team.

Development-based Intervention:

Whenever possible, artistic and cultural elements have been integrated into the children's education. Topics like the culture of peace, and human and cultural rights are addressed through participatory games and sports. Children thus develop the ability to understand other peoples' realities, express their feelings, construct their identities, and develop dreams and aspirations. Such activities have provided an organised space for the children to act in a democratic manner, i.e. to co-operate, respect others, and voice opinions and concerns in the form of group dialogue. Street plays have played a very important role in generating awareness on children's rights and the importance of children's education. Drawing, painting and craftwork has also given children an avenue to improve interpersonal and communication skills. The children have gained self-confidence and they have learned to trust others.

Observation notes:
Solas campaign against child labour

Street corner activism

Nov. 18th 2009 – Street Corner Campaign

In it's second year, the Solas campaign against child labour is becoming a prominent event in Kolkata's calendar of events. The name Solas means 'light' in the Irish language. It is comprised of two days of action against child labour and child abuse. Actions taken include street cornering, a door-to-door campaign in housing complexes and campaigns at shopping malls.

I visited all three 'street corners' throughout Kolkata. At each were several teachers and volunteers, and children from HOPE schools resplendent in their uniforms. There was plenty of noisy music and entertainers like clowns, magicians and ventriloquists. Each of these acts conveyed the message that children needed to go to school to improve their chances in life. The party atmosphere attracted members of the public to take a look. They put up posters espousing the HOPE messages of health, education and equality for children. Accompanying these were posters drawn by the children themselves on the same issues. I found these in particular quite powerful. They also asked the public sign their petition. It is remarkably difficult to even find a spot to set up something like this among the chaotic traffic, noise, dust and fumes that is daily life on Kolkata's streets. However, they did manage against great odds. They were allowed to proceed without any problem by the police. I found a terrible contrast between the healthy little HOPE children and the poor little barefoot children from the streets who came along for a look.

A soldier signs a petition against child labour

Annemarie with the boys from Howrah Drop In Centre

Children are given a voice

Maureen with some HOPE staff

HOPE children with banners

Nov.19th, 2009 - Street Rally

A rally was held in the city centre, with the full co-operation of the police. An estimated 2,000 people marched through the city carrying banners against child labour in all areas. There was a party atmosphere, with everybody carrying colourful flags, pictures, banners and balloons. The Irish volunteers helped the children to paint pictures of butterflies, flowers and other cheerful images to evoke the happy childhood that is lost by child labourers in the streets, in hotels and in private homes. Leading the march were Maureen along with Paulami, HOPE projects manager, and the one who spearheaded this campaign. Joining them were several Bengali celebrities from the field of sports and drama. There was quite a bit of media interest. The marchers were comprised of the children that HOPE helps and houses and the staff, both paid and voluntary, who help to keep the HOPE show on the road. The young Irish volunteers were also out in force, adding another dimension to the proceedings. Their positive spirit is infectious. Everybody wore T-shirts, wristbands and sun-visors bearing the HOPE logo and also that of the Solas campaign itself. There was plenty of singing, generating a cheerful atmosphere. Following this, a seminar was held at the prominent Rotary Club where guests were invited to speak as part of a panel discussion.

Some of the children's artwork

HOPE children enjoying a snack

HOPE children enjoying a snack

Maureen with a group of staff and celebrities as the rally kicks off

Marching through central Kolkata

Irish volunteers: Lindsay Wolford, Mary Gormley, Eoin Fahey, Eoin MacCormaic, Ben Brooks, Kelly Campbell, Kate Cotter

Maureen addresses Seminar on Child Labour at the Rotary Club, Kolkata

HOPE PROTECTION HOMES FOR CHILDREN			
HKF	111 Girls	BPWT	25 HIV Infected and Affected Children
	54 Boys	ABWU	22 Girls – Midway Home
	34 Rehabilitated Addicted Boys	SEED	36 Girls
PBKOJP	17 Girls	HRLN	15 Girls

Many, many thousands of families and children have made the streets of Kolkata their home. Estimates vary as to their numbers – perhaps it is as many as 250,000. They live in over 200 different pockets of the city where they eat, sleep, work and grow up. For these children every day is a battle: for food, for shelter and for the right to survive. They have been forced by extreme poverty to do anything they possibly can to survive – rag picking, begging, petty crime. Deprived even of very basic nutrition, never mind health, education and shelter, their problems are a bottomless pit.

To address these serious problems, the Hope Foundation works with local NGOs and runs protection homes for street children and vulnerable at-risk children. Many of the children have been physically and psychologically abused, victims of sexual abuse and trafficking, and all are in desperate need of guidance and support. HOPE wants to break the cycle of poverty and free them from a life of fear and destitution.

As well as their own homes, HOPE also funds the work of four other partner NGOs in Kolkata who run similar homes. These are all well-established and respected organisations in the city.

Hope Kolkata Foundation itself runs four homes for vulnerable children, one for boys and two for girls, and one for ex drug-addicted boys. The homes provide a healing touch to **traumatised children** who have faced acute loneliness and helplessness on the streets. In the Homes these children receive:

- 24- hour care
- Shelter
- Clothing
- Education,
- Health care and insurance,
- Counselling
- Various recreation choices (yoga, swimming, dance, drawing, excursions)
- Life skills training.

Panditya Girl's Home

Panditya Girl's Home was the first HOPE residential home, established in 1999. It was funded by Mairéad Sorensen, Butler's Chocolates and the HOPE Dublin Committee. 44 girls live here. Jenny Browne and Annemarie Murray also live in simple rooms

Annemarie Murray outside the Panditya Girl's Home

on the top floor of this building. This is also where Maureen Forrest stays when she is in Kolkata. They are therefore available all the time in the event of any emergency. It is also the location of the Hope Kolkata Foundation Head Office, and the office of its Director, Geeta Venkadakrishnan.

interview...

Geeta Venkadakrishnan,
Director, HOPE Kolkata Foundation

"All children are diamonds that just need to be shone"

Geeta Venkadakrishnan, in front of a map of her beloved Kolkata

Geeta, originally from Kerala, used to work with CINI (Child in Need Institute). Maureen sponsored a child at their NGO and came to visit the child in 1997-98. She recognised immediately that Maureen was "a glowing diamond". She visited a slum while here and was very upset when she saw the conditions. She wanted to personally sponsor more children, when she saw so many of them starving and living in filthy slums. She made contact with SPAN to find out more. Then she had the idea to set up HOPE and asked Geeta to join her, along with Pushpa, Frank, the driver, and Feroza, a caregiver in the Boy's Home. They started out with fourteen children and Geeta can remember all of their names. One died of cardiac problems despite three operations in Ireland, and his picture still adorns the little multi-denominational shrine at Panditya. She lists off the success stories of the rest – they are all working in banks, hotels, as teachers, and one set up his own NGO and is married to a girl who was also raised in the HOPE Girl's Home.

The children go to government schools and some to private boarding schools. Sometimes teachers single out "the HOPE kids", i.e. poor, and don't call them by name. They send counsellors to talk to the teachers to make sure the children are not stigmatised. The children constantly ask questions as to why their parents do not take care of them, or why they were abused. They need constant counselling, which, she says, is "like a daily food". She always stresses the intelligence and resilience of the children.

However, the children feel very insecure and are constantly looking for a sense of connection, a home and a love of their own. When they become adolescents, they constantly search for true love. They counsel the girls to be careful and take it slow. They come from backgrounds of family conflict, living in overcrowded slums where a big family shares one tiny room where there is no privacy. Sometimes they are sent to live with extended family where they are treated cruelly or abused. They are very traumatised children. As adolescents, they might meet a boy whose family doesn't want the girl because she is poor and has no family. She says their work is "99 per cent successful". They give the children unconditional love and she says that she treats the HOPE children the same as her own children at home. They provide bank accounts, medical insurance, celebrate birthdays and take them on excursions. The caregivers sleep in the same room as the children, as that closeness is an integral part of Indian culture.

HKF is a direct implementing agency of HOPE Ireland. HKF employs 200 staff, both full time and part time, including counsellors, lawyers and doctors. As well as the three homes, they run outreach programmes, crèches, coaching centres, eleven mobile clinics, health programmes, the detox program for drug addicts, vocational training, the hospital, childwatch ambulances, Nabadishas, networking with other NGOs, advocacy on human rights and fundraising.

They support the entire extended family of the people they help. They sponsor their medical care and get jobs for the children's mothers, for example, as ward 'ayahs', or carers, at hospital. They also run crèches for the children of fruit and vegetable sellers. The children are protected from having to work and from being trafficked. They have coaching centres and sometimes literacy classes for adults, as their involvement leads to an improvement in their dropout rates. They have monthly meetings with parents to see what they need. They might need a detox centre for an addict, or need to know what resources they can access. They empower them and inform them of their rights, and also educate mothers on children's rights.

They have sex education programmes for adolescents and workshops on keeping their bodies clean and safe, how to "protect and protest", to report any abuse. They have counsellors as well as peer educator groups. They have Community Health Volunteers (CHVs) who do outreach work in the slums. The goal is that this will help to empower the children to protest and report abuse. The peer groups will keep their eyes and ears open, so they have a 'chain system'. Each group of CHVs has 4 men, 4 women and 4 adolescents. They are all trained in child protection procedures – everyone "from driver to director" knows how to file incident reports and abuse reports.

Geeta with Maureen

They have a big problem with child marriage in general, but mostly among Muslims. Their families view them as ready for marriage after menstruation starts. Marriage is illegal before 18 for girls and 21 for boys. They threaten them with the law and they have intervened to stop a lot of marriages. Sometimes girls want to go ahead, but social workers try to persuade them to wait.

In the slums, most girls would have their first baby at 18 or 19, and then they have 4-7 children. Breastfeeding works as a natural contraceptive, spacing out the children. The give them the Pill (OCP), and if the women are illiterate, they educate them through coloured charts and diagrams in the clinics. They put them in touch with a family contraceptive organisation too to arrange for sterilisation if they so wish.

Many of the slum children were never registered at birth, so they have no birth certificates. They advise them and help them to register, and health workers will go with them to help. They raise consciousness among them as to their entitlements, to "try and ensure institutional delivery" in health and education.

She says that the abandonment of families by men is very common: they have a family, then up and leave. They might move around between construction sites, as they live on them while work goes on. It is always a trauma for the families. In most cases, the marriage is not registered as legal, so they have no papers. It is very common even among the middle class, to have a marriage just based on trust.

Babies are sometimes stolen for adoptions agencies. It is common for the middle class and the rich to have problems conceiving. Perhaps after an abortion or after taking the Pill for a long time, they might have polycysts on their ovaries. The 'middle man' in these cases can get Rs. 6,000 for a girl or up to Rs. 25,000 for a boy.

The discrimination against girls and women is very severe among the poor in India. Girl children are "much less priority" and boys have "all the advantages". When a girl is born, parents start saving at birth both for the girl's dowry and for their own old age, because the girl will marry and join another family. There are all sorts of forms of exploitation. Middle class and rich people often hire girls as domestic labourers and babysitters. They are often not paid, just getting 'clothes and food'. They are frequently physically or sexually abused. It is also common that when families get into debt, men will pimp out their wives, forcing them to have sex with strangers.

Counsellor, Sruti Kar, beside her chart with stars for positive reinforcement.

Chatting to Geeta is so fascinating that one could sit there easily for 24 hours listening to her. She has so much experience and so much knowledge, that the stories just pour out of her. She has a huge heart and also a huge amount of courage – nothing fazes her. With this woman at the helm, the future of Hope Kolkata Foundation is bright.

Life stories of some of the girls at Panditya:

Profile...

Mongola (23)

Mongola has been living at the HOPE home since the beginning. She was born in the red-light area of Kolkata. She never knew her father and her mother died when she was very young, and a group of sex workers took responsibility for raising her. She was alone at that age for a whole year until a kind lady picked her up and brought her to a home. She saved her from a life on the streets, robbing from shops and eating out of rubbish piles. She has been at Panditya since she was young, from where she attended state school all throughout the years. She has now finished and she is doing a computer course so that she can get "a proper job in an office". There are no other girls her own age at the home now, so she says she feels a bit lonely sometimes. The others have moved out to houses and are working. She hopes to join them soon. She says HOPE is very good for children, because to get higher education helps them to get qualified and to get settled in their lives. She is very interested in her studies. A look of dread passes over her face when asked to imagine if HOPE hadn't rescued her from the streets.

Sobha (27)

Sobha lived on the pavement with her father, who was a van rickshaw puller and her mother, who has psychiatric problems. The family is extremely poor, and her mother has been unable to raise the children. Because of poverty, she was sent out to beg for food and money at a temple and on the streets. Sobha moved to a hostel in 2003 and stayed there until 2006, so that she could complete her 3rd level studies. She then moved to the HOPE home. Her brother and sister are also both in HOPE homes. Her father now works in the HOPE Hospital as he had bad asthma and couldn't work much longer as a rickshaw puller. Sobha is a responsible girl who takes good care of her family to the best of her ability. She pays her parents' rent even though she is also trying to build her own life. She is extremely grateful for everything that HOPE has done for her throughout her life.

Parveen (25)

"HOPE is my mother and father – they gave me life".

Parveen is a happy, responsible young woman who works fulltime in the tailoring unit and Life Skills shop. She has been living at Panditya Girl's Home since it began in 1999. Her history, however, is one of violence, abuse and illness. She was born in a village at the edge of the city. Her father took a second wife and her mother moved out. They came to stay on the platform at Sealdah train station and they survived by begging and selling vegetables that they had previously stolen. She endured beatings and threats from various men during this time. She was sold into marriage at the age of about 14. The marriage was a disaster, as her husband in turn tried to sell her into a brothel in a red-light district. Her experience there proved very traumatic for her and had long lasting effects on her life. She was subsequently brought to CINI-ASHA Girl's Home, where she got all the necessary treatment. Eventually she came to live at the HOPE home full-time. However, she has now moved out and is renting a house with her sister who is currently in college. Her rent is 1,200 rupees per month, which she pays as her sister is not earning at the moment. She is waiting for her sister to graduate and start earning before looking for a husband. She gets some support through the HOPE sponsorship programme.

A (11)

A lived on the pavements of Sudder St. in Kolkata with her father. A has a speech difficulty. Her father is a beggar who earns about Rs. 500 per month. He took advantage of A's disability by forcing her to beg. She suffered beatings from her father when she failed to bring money to him. Her mother stayed in her own home in a slum. The HOPE Childwatch team found A in a traumatic state one night. She had been severely beaten by her father. The team rescued her from there and she was placed in the HOPE Girl's Home.

L (18)

L is from a slum near the HOPE office. She was living with her maternal grandmother. Her mother is a sex worker by profession and she refused to keep her daughter. She has always done housework at home, as well as working as a maidservant. She was also expected to take care of her cousins, sisters and brothers. She is a soft-spoken and very friendly girl. She is very responsible and loves to take care of others. She is very faithful and trustworthy.

J (14)

J lived in Tollygunge slum by the railway. She has six sisters. She and her three sisters are in the HOPE home. Her mother died in 2003 of TB and a year later her father also died of TB. Her mother gave birth to a baby girl shortly before she died, and that baby was adopted. Her elder sister had been missing since then. After her parents died, the younger sister took responsibility for caring for the younger siblings. Then J started working as a maidservant in a home to support her sisters. The 2 younger sisters were sent to the HIVe crèche and another sister R was sent to the Preparatory centre. R and her siblings were detected with TB. HIVe referred J and her other siblings to the HOPE Girl's Home and they were all given the necessary treatment and placed in the HOPE Home.

T (Aged 12)

T lived in the state of Bihar with her father and stepmother. Unable to bear the torture inflicted upon her by her stepmother, she ran away from home and took a train to Howrah station in Kolkata. Here a handicapped lady extended a helping hand to her and gave her work in a small hotel. She started staying with this lady on the pavement at Howrah. There was no protection for T during the night, while she slept at the station. One day, the HOPE Childwatch team found her at the station in a traumatised state. They rescued her from there and placed her in the HOPE Girl's Home. She is a very lovable girl, who is always ready to help others.

Random notes from the girls' files:

- D contracted severe diarrhoea and was admitted to a state hospital. She was given an injection and due to hospital negligence, the syringe broke in her left hand and was never removed which led to gangrene, and her left hand had to be amputated.
- Two of her brothers died when they were babies due to the mother's neglect. M's mother, who is an alcoholic, took to begging. As a result, M was quite a neglected child as her mother showed little interest in her upbringing.

Asida shows me where she sleeps

The girls draw some pictures

Board full of cheerful pictures of the girls

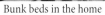

Bunk beds in the home

The little multi-denominational shrine in the prayer room

Kasba Girl's Home

Kasba Girl's Home currently houses 67 girls. The Louis and Zelie Foundation funded its purchase and it opened in 2007. It provides residential care, educational coaching, counselling, healthcare, yoga, games, art, drama and dance.

interview...

Pushpa Basu,
Housemother at both Kasba and Panditya

Pushpa Basu, Housemother
[Kelly Campbell]

Kasba Girl's Home

Pushpa is the housemother at both Kasba and Panditya. She is also on the Board of Directors. Before joining HOPE, she used to work at another charity, CINI-ASHA. There she met Maureen and started to work at HOPE homes. This selfless woman started working as a housemother during the daytime only, but it became obvious that she needed to stay in the homes on a residential 24-hour basis. She says she has a very understanding husband and three grown up children. She sleeps in both homes – she never really knows where she will sleep each night. She literally doesn't even have her own bed. She just sleeps anywhere that is available and is on site 24/7 to deal with emergencies. She does home visits too, going out to needy children in the slums, on the streets and in the stations.

She says that a big problem is when the children, especially girls, want to drop out of school early and their guardians want them to marry young, at the age of 14 or 15. "When that happens, I feel bad, like I'm a failure", she says. They send in counsellors to talk to parents and they have monthly meetings to try to convince them not to send daughters into early marriage and to let them continue with school. They have a very low dropout rate. They try to give the children options, to convince them that they can make choices about their lives. Suparna is the counsellor at Kasba.

Pushpa showed me her 'family album' of the children. She keeps a record of them when they were first admitted to the homes with their parents or guardians. They are all in a poor state at this stage, many malnourished, neglected and possibly abused. Sometimes a whole family might be taken in and given medical care if needed.

"I love the organisation, I love the children"

"There are so many needy, tortured children. Why not give them a chance?"

"They need proper food, proper education - we want to give them a good life"

Pushpa shows me her 'family album' of the girls

Attempts might be made to get the parents a job and children might be taken in to the homes. One mother in the pictures was skeletal, as she was dying of AIDS. She was brought to Arunima hospice where she later died, and her two girls kept at Kasba Girl's Home. Pushpa was as proud of each child's achievements as if she had given birth to each one herself. She also has an album of each child on her birthday with her cake and candles and all her friends around her. They update the album annually.

Some of the girls having their lunch

Time for lessons

Chart of the girls' achievements

Breakfast time

Volunteer Alicia Banbury at work at the crèche

Nap time

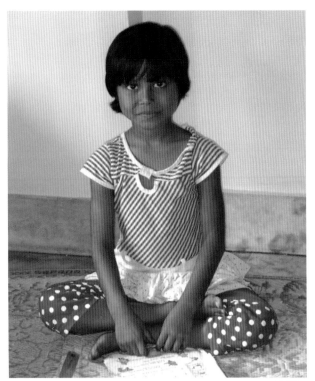
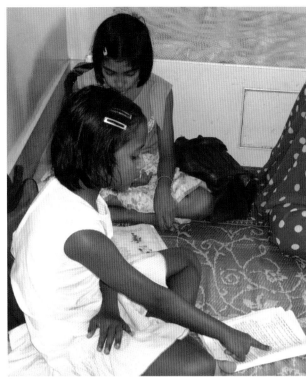

Children at lessons

The girls in their pyjamas ready for bed [Kelly Campbell]

P (13)

P stayed with her parents on Golpark pavement in Kolkata. Both her parents are rag pickers, earning Rs. 700-800 per month. P had to face a lot of violence in her family, as her father was an alcoholic and used to beat her up. The care she received was very poor. She started rag picking along with her mother, work she disliked very much. Later on, the HOPE Childwatch team identified her and brought her to the HOPE Girl's Home. She is gradually becoming more self-sufficient now, and getting more interested in her studies.

T (14)

When T was 5, her father died, after which her family's economic situation worsened. They were forced to live on the pavements near Ruby Hospital in Kolkata. Their only source of income was rag picking, earning only Rs. 20-30 per day. This area was not at all safe for a young girl. A local lady gave her mother HOPE's contact number. T was placed in the HOPE Girl's Home after verification and home visits. She is an introverted child with few close friends. She loves to study and other extracurricular activities. Her adjustment capacity is high.

M (13)

M lived with her parents and sister. Her mother has cancer and she is undergoing treatment at a cancer hospital. Her father, a paddy field worker earning Rs. 800 per month, is an alcoholic and is unconcerned about his family. Her mother, despite being ill, begged on the street to support the family's basic needs. There have been days when M didn't get to eat at all. She couldn't continue her education, as it was not possible for her mother to buy her schoolbooks. Her mother learned about HOPE from another NGO while she was in hospital, and M was placed in a HOPE home. Her sister has been placed in a boarding school sponsored by HOPE.

S (6)

She lived with her parents in a rural village. Her mother was regularly tortured and beaten by her father, a rickshaw van puller who earns Rs. 800 per month. In March 2007, he poured petrol on her and burned her whole body. This terrible suffering inflicted on her mother was all because of her dowry. T witnessed this and she was locked in a room for one month in her home by her father and given only the basics for survival. Later on her family came to know about this and sought the help of a Bengali news channel, along with the help of HKF Childwatch team and the police, for her rescue. She is now placed in the HOPE Girl's Home and her mother is placed in a nursing home, and HOPE is paying for her treatment.

Random lines from the girls' files:

- She arrived at HOPE very malnourished and covered with skin disease.
- Her mother has psychiatric problems and she was very neglected.
- Her mother was often in a traumatised state from the beatings and couldn't look after her family.
- She was exposed to all forms of abuse and neglect.

The Boy's Home

The Boy's Home is open since November 2005, and has been funded by John Ronan of Treasury Holdings. It provides residential care, counselling, educational coaching, healthcare, yoga and games. 55 little boys live here.

The Boy's Home

The boys come in from school

The ground floor of the Boy's Home doubles as an office for staff, including Jenny, the Overseas Director and Paulami, Projects Manager. There is always a happy buzz of children playing and laughing in the background. When coming and going to school, the boys troupe through the office with cheery calls of "Morning, Aunty" and Morning, Uncle". It makes for a very personal atmosphere when the work of running the charity operates from within the same building as where the children live.

It is heart-warming to see these little boys in a safe, clean and loving home. They all have devastatingly sad backgrounds, which one can only guess at until you read their files, with their litany of disasters. HOPE is quite literally a lifeline for these children.

In their files, their official address is registered as a particular stretch of pavement, a railway or a bus shelter. Many have migrated from rural areas or Bangladesh. Many parents are ill, or die, or children are left with poor and old grandparents who cannot care for them.

There is such a contrast between seeing the happy smiling little boys and the horrendous life circumstances they have left. Their lives have been marked with abuse, destitution, violence, forced migration, abandonment and illness. They have a fantastic spirit of survival, despite their destitute backgrounds.

interview...

Supriyo Roy
Counsellor, Boys Home

"We say to the boys - you are here to make your own future"

"Sometimes the difference between their parents and HOPE care-givers is the same as between hell and heaven"

"They love it here"

Counsellor Supriyo Roy

Supriyo, the genial counsellor at the boy's home has an M.Phil in Clinical Psychology. He says that the boys suffer from "emotional emptiness" because of the hard lives they have lived. They may have no parents at all, or have been raised by a single parent or by grandparents. The lives of the pavement-dwellers are usually the hardest, as they usually have experience of alcoholism, drug abuse, violence and abuse. They are sometimes hyperactive as they are not aware of how to express their emotions in a healthy way. He lets them know that they can tell him absolutely anything, that they can explore their emotions and share their memories with him. He provides them with support and comfort.

It can take time to build trust and they have a great fear of abandonment. The previous counsellor left and he replaced him this year. The first question the boys asked him was "how long will you stay?" They have a huge fear of rejection as that is all they have experienced. They feel angry with their parents but he tries to explain to them why things had to happen the way they did. They also maintain contact with the parents or guardians if at all possible, and let them go 'home' for holidays and festivals if they wish.

The boys feel lonely sometimes. Jealousy is a common emotion, but they combat this by creating cohesiveness through group activities. They also have exercises in peer leadership and education. They let the boys be the leader of a group, to maintain tidiness, doing homework and good behaviour, for a week at a time. They try to teach them responsibility, especially as they become teenagers. They reinforce positive behaviour and teach them about how you need to compete and work hard to achieve well and be celebrated on the wall charts. These are life lessons indeed.

Study time

One little boy shows me all his worldly belongings

Lunch time

Boys will be boys!

The boys watch some cartoons on TV

G (8)

G stayed with his parents and sister on the pavement in Gariahat. His father, a day labourer, is an alcoholic and beat up his wife regularly. The pavement dwellers of Gariahat were evicted due to road works, and this meant that the family had to move. Childwatch referred G to the Boy's Home where he came to live, after talking with his parents. He has been here for 4 years.

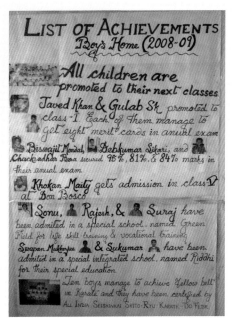

Chart of boys' achievements

D (7)

His parents are separated and he lived with his mother and sister on the pavement near Kalighat. He and his sister were left alone by day, when his mother went to work as a rag picker. He was found wandering alone, looking for food, by HIVe Night watch. He was referred to the Boy's Home and his mother was contacted. His sister now stays at the Girl's Home and his mother now works as a maidservant and stays in this home. D has been at the Boy's Home for 3.5 years.

S (6)

S lived with his parents and one elder sister, having migrated from Bangladesh. Their economic condition is v poor, earning money by begging or rag picking. His mother suffers from asthma and his father is also very weak. S can't get proper care, guidance or nutrition from his parents. His mother contacted Howrah drop-in centre for her son's rehabilitation. Through that centre, he was placed in the Boy's Home, where he has been for 1 year.

R (7)

R is an orphan child who lived on Park St. footpath, as a child labourer and beggar. He and his brother lived in L. but his brother became a drug addict and he had to resort to begging. His brother was rescued by another NGO and brought to Mukti detox centre. R was rescued from Park St. pavement by BPWT and he was brought to HOPE to live.

S (Age 3)

His father left his family a few years ago. His mother had worked as a domestic helper, but she developed some mental health problems and her behaviour meant that her neighbours locked her up. She is now receiving treatment and is deemed unfit to mind her children. He was severely malnourished when he came to the Boy's Home.

S (10)

S has cerebral palsy and is also deaf and dumb. He was found at Tollygunge railway station by the police, who contacted HIVe, and he was then referred to the Boy's Home four years ago. His mother died and his father married again. His stepmother tortured and beat him, and he wandered away because of this cruel treatment.

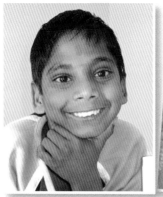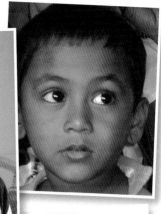

Random lines from the boys' case files:

- His mother is a vegetable seller, whose monthly income is Rs. 500.
- His mother left him and became a sex worker for survival.
- He starts crying if we ask him about his family members.
- His father is a rickshaw puller, whose income is Rs. 500 per month.
- His father is addicted to drugs and was violent in the home.
- He ran away from his home due to beatings.
- His mother had mental health problems and is unable to look after her children properly.
- His mother is a beggar, whose income is Rs. 30-40 a day.
- He never had a chance to know what a normal childhood is because of domestic violence at home.
- He grew up on the pavement in a state of neglect.
- His father died of AIDS.

Programme for the Rehabilitation of Young Drug Addicts

Drug abuse is often an underestimated problem for young people in India. Kolkata's Howrah Station, one of the biggest railway stations in Asia, sees approximately one million commuters a day and has become a shelter for many homeless people. In Howrah people can make a living by taking on various small jobs; looking for recyclables, carrying luggage, setting up and working at food stalls and inevitably some thieving. Solvent abuse is a widespread problem amongst the children who lives at Howrah. Drugs help them to escape from the realities of their lives and survive yet another day. As they are often high throughout the day, many children have accidents as they are caught under the railways. Many lose limbs or have massive scars that bear testament to their hard lives.

In 2005, HOPE started a Rehabilitation and Intervention Programme for the boys from Howrah station. It was designed and co-ordinated by K. Viswanath. He met Maureen and the HOPE team in Tamil Nadu in 2005 during the aid and rescue efforts after the tsunami.

This programme has five phases:
- The **first** is the Drop-In Centre at Howrah station. The railway children of Howrah can come to the centre for support, get food and attend some classes
- The **second** is attendance at Mukti Detoxification Centre in order to 'get clean'
- The **third** is moving into Punorjibon Rehabilitation Home
- The **fourth** is semi-independent living, where HOPE still provide some support
- The **fifth** is fully independent living, when the boys are fully functioning adults.

The programme aims to:
- Rehabilitate children after detoxification to lead a drug-free life
- Place the children in formal schools/ hostels
- Provide vocational training
- Provide jobs through referrals
- Support the individuals towards independent living.

Howrah Drop-In Centre

The Drop-in Centre is co-ordinated by Mr. And Mrs. Chatterjee. They use a tiny space the size of a garden shed in a run-down abandoned area of the massive Howrah station. They deal with about fifty drug-addicted children, from 8.30am to 6pm every day. They run a primary healthcare clinic here as

The boys at the Drop-in Centre at Howrah

The boys at the Drop-in Centre at Howrah

well. These children (mostly boys) ride the trains to collect recyclables, mainly water bottles. They may also be involved in petty crime. Ninety per cent of them are addicted to an industrial glue called Dendrite (which costs Rs.17 per packet), while many also smoke marijuana and drink alcohol. They are mostly orphans who come from all over the country on the trains. They might earn Rs. 50-200 per day. What they do is dangerous and many of them have lost an arm or leg. Also, they get a lot of harassment from the police. The police can get away with this, as these runaways do not exist officially. There is no place for them to stay overnight, so every day the staff at the drop in centre has to start from scratch with them. The staff do not see much progress, so the work can be disheartening. However, the boys from Punorjibon come here as part of a peer educator programme, talking to the boys and trying to convince them to get clean. Many do not want to because they would have to endure a structured and disciplined regime, which would be a new experience for them after their rough but free-wheeling life. However, if they are motivated enough, the next phase of this rehab programme is available to them – to go for complete detoxification.

One boy who is an amputee

Mukti Rehabilitation Centre:

Serenity Prayer

*God, grant me the serenity
To accept the things I cannot change,
The courage to change the things I can,
and the wisdom to know the difference.*

interview...

Sandip Mukherjee, Farouk Ahmed, Vishwanath

Mukti Substance Abuse Counsellors

Mukti substance abuse counsellors, Sandip Mukherjee and Farouk Ahmed with Vishwanath, Secretary of Mukti

The slogan of Mukti Rehabilitation Centre is 'From Bondage to Freedom'. This 30-bed clinic is a detoxification centre for drug addicts. There are not too many centres like this available anywhere in India, and only a few private clinics in the whole country.

HOPE funds the children who have come through their own programme from Howrah. It costs Rs. 250 a day, i.e. Rs. 7,500 a month per person. However, the addicts treated there are, according to Vishwanath, "an assorted crowd", meaning that they come from all walks of life, all classes and creeds. Depending on their means, sometimes the addicts themselves might pay their own bills for their treatment.

They operate according to the Narcotics Anonymous 12 Steps programme. Everyone is treated equally, and nobody wants to know the addict's personal history or what level of status one enjoys in society. The only identity they have is their first name and that they are an addict. This is especially hard in a status-obsessed, hierarchical society like India. They use a 'therapeutic community concept' that has an equalising effect, with everyone striving together towards a common goal. They encourage them to express their feelings and emotions. Three indispensable spiritual principles are honesty, open-mindedness and willingness. They see the process as a rebirth, that recovering addicts are like toddlers learning how to walk for the first time. They have a 35 per cent full recovery rate, which they say is very good by international standards. They also do outreach work mainly at the train stations (Howrah and Sealdah) where the addicts can find food and shelter.

The main drug is 'brown sugar', which is an adulterated, 'cut' version of heroin. Pure heroin is very rare. The average cost of maintaining this drug habit might be Rs.150 a day. They can smoke it or inject it without much risk of overdose because it is so impure. The heroin comes in from the Golden

Crescent (Pakistan, Afghanistan) and the Golden Triangle (Myanmar, Laos, Thailand). Cocaine is rare as it is too expensive and they are not in the right supply routes for it. The solvents they use are Dendrite glue (which contains benzene, a carcinogen), and correction fluid, diluted down with something like nail polish remover. They also use cough syrup and painkillers, as it is very easy to get anything from pharmacists over the counter in India. Interestingly, they completely reject the use of methadone as a replacement for heroin, because that just contains social problems without treating the reasons for the addiction. As part of his rehab, each addict will sometimes be given the responsibility to lead a therapy session.

The withdrawal symptoms from brown sugar are not as severe as they would be from pure heroin. They can get bad stomach cramps, for which they give them mild drugs to treat and relieve symptoms. These are given in the first week and gradually weaned off so that they are on no drugs at all after fifteen days. If they need it, a psychiatrist might be brought in and he can administer drugs if needed, or a doctor in case of medical problems. The detoxification period is fifteen days, and the recommended stay is three months, but on average, but they usually stay for about two months.

Vishwanath is the Secretary of Mukti. He, along with both of the full time substance abuse counsellors is an ex-addicts himself. As he says, "I have direct experience, not vicarious experience". The men think that this helps them to empathise with their clients. While it is not, of course, 100 per cent necessary, they say that it helps them to get "in congruence with people's feelings".

CASE MANAGEMENT RECORD
(MARCH-2002 ——-MARCH-2009)

SL.NO	PARTICULARS	NO.OF CLIENTS
1.	NO.OF ADMISSION	1037
2.	NO.OF DISCHARGE	968
3.	DROP OUT	22
4.	NEW CASES	420
5.	OLD CASES	617

AGE-WISE BREAK-UP

1.	11 yrs – 20 yrs	144
2.	21 yrs – 30 yrs	413
3.	31 yrs – 40 yrs	302
4.	41 yrs - 50 yrs	145
5.	51 yrs – 60 yrs	33

OCCUPATION OF CLIENTS

1.	EMPLOYED/SERVICE	200
2.	UNEMPLOYED	536
3.	BUSINESS	244
4.	STUDENT	57

MARITAL STATUS

1.	MARRIED	436
2.	UNMARRIED	515
3.	DIVORCED/SEPARATED	86

LITERACY STANDARD

1.	ILLITERATE	149
2.	NON-MATRICULATE	328
3.	MATRICULATE	152
4.	HIGHER SECONDARY	196
5.	GRADUATE	173
6.	POST GRADUATE	39

SUBSTANCE ABUSED

1.	BROWN SUGAR	607
2.	ALCOHOL	160
3.	CANABIS	80
4.	COUGH-SYRUP/PILLS	86
5.	SOLVENTS/MULTIPLE/IDU	104

A record of the addicts who come to Mukti

DAILY TIME SCHEDULE

7:00 A.M	WAKE UP
7:15 A.M	MORNING TEA / SELF CLEANING
8:00 A.M	HOUSE CLEANING
9:00 A.M	MEDICATION / BREAKFAST
10:00 A.M	MORNING DEVOTION
11:00 A.M	DOCTOR'S CHECK UP / TEA
11:30 A.M	BATHING
1:00 P.M	MEDICATION / LUNCH
2:00 P.M	LEISURE TIME / COUNSELLING
4:30 P.M	INPUT SESSION (MONDAY – FRIDAY)
5:30 P.M	FUN TIME / COUNSELLING
7:00 P.M	GROUP DISCUSSION (MONDAY – FRIDAY)
9:00 P.M	MEDICATION / DINNER
10:00 P.M	LIGHTS OUT
4:30 P.M	NA / AA MEETINGS (SATURDAY)
SUNDAY	TIME SCHEDULE OFF

The schedule followed at Mukti Rehab Centre

Narcotics Anonymous Twelve Steps
These are the principles that made our recovery possible:

1. We admitted that we were powerless over our addiction, that our lives had become unmanageable.

2. We came to believe that a Power greater than ourselves could restore us to sanity.

3. We made a decision to turn our will and our lives over to the care of God as we understood Him.

4. We made a searching and fearless moral inventory of ourselves.

5. We admitted to God, to ourselves, and to another human being the exact nature of our wrongs.

6. We were entirely ready to have God remove all these defects of character.

7. We humbly asked Him to remove our shortcomings.

8. We made a list of all persons we had harmed, and became willing to make amends to them all.

9. We made direct amends to such people wherever possible, except when to do so would injure them or others.

10. We continued to take personal inventory and when we were wrong promptly admitted it.

11. We sought through prayer and meditation to improve our conscious contact with God as we understood Him, praying only for knowledge of His will for us and the power to carry that out.

12. Having had a spiritual awakening as a result of these steps, we tried to carry this message to addicts, and to practice these principles in all our affairs.

Punorjibon Boy's Home

Punorjibon (meaning 'rebirth') is a residential home for past drug addicted boys from Howrah station. It exists since August 2005 and its purchase and running costs were funded by Mrs. Eileen McCarthy, Ovens, Co. Cork, Blackrock College and IMPACT. They moved into their new premises in 2007. Services available here include the rehabilitation programme, educational support, woodwork, electrical training, photography, sports, job placements and a follow-up programme. It has room for twenty children, but there are currently sixteen boys in residence, with four more due to go to Mukti from Howrah station, having been encouraged by counsellors to get clean. Many of the boys are there on a long-term basis. Some boys might stay for two or three years, and can come from inside or outside the state. There is also a crisis intervention centre here where some of the poor are brought in and cared for. For example, there is one old man

Plaque to donor

there at present and they are trying to find a place for him in a more appropriate home. All medical needs are addressed, for example, one boy has recently had brain surgery at a cost of Rs. 80,000. He would never have had access to such medical care without the Hope Foundation.

The boys playing their favourite board game

Punorjibon Rehabilitation Home

interview...

K. Vishwanath
Director of the Rehabilitation Programme

Vishwanath

The atmosphere at Punorjibon is very friendly, loving and relaxed. The children wander in and out of Vishwanath's office. He is like their father, addressing all their little concerns. One broke his sandal and needed it fixed, another needed money to go to the gym, another boy brought me some sweets he wanted me to try, another joked that I had a haircut like a boy. There is a friendly, relaxed atmosphere. I saw one little boy who was playing with some beads sitting in the near dark. Vishwanath told him to get up and put on the electric light. He was only there 6 weeks, and was used to such a tough environment, he would never have dared to do this on his own.

Many of the boys have had accidents on the rail tracks, perhaps having fallen in front of the trains. There are several amputees among the boys. They have endured massive traumas in their lives and are damaged physically and psychologically. When they move here first, the boys have huge insecurities and find it very hard to trust anyone.

"Gaining trust takes time", says Vishwanath. There can be mood swings and impulsive behaviour. Addicts are used to instant gratification and these boys are used to freedom and autonomy at the stations and discipline of any kind is hard for them to accept at first. Also, they have usually left families in abject poverty and may not want to go home. They might give a false name and counsellors tell them they won't be forced to go back if they do not want to, but convincing them of this can be hard.

If their behaviour is inappropriate, counsellors address it, either in individual or group sessions. In time, the change of lifestyle can change their attitude to drugs, and they are helped in this with counselling. Rehabilitation needs compassion, care and skills. When they are treated with respect and cared for, they will then want to stay. Vishwanath says that it is very important that the child himself has to see the need for it, that he is not just doing it to please the caregivers or anyone else. So it is all about each individual's motivation, and nobody can be forced to do something they do not really want to do. Some of the boys' stories illustrate this:

- One boy got a job in a restaurant, earned Rs. 600 a month (very low pay). He could make more at the station, yet he wanted to stay, because he felt safer and that he was respected for the first time ever. He couldn't keep the money at the station because of drug use and having to pay off the guards and hardened criminals who extorted money for him.

- One boy had a festered sore on his leg that he got in a burn when he was small. They fixed him up and it healed eventually. He then kept scratching it so that it came back and then he ran away. He saw it as his source of income for begging, which he viewed as a more secure future.

They have to be trained as to their entitlements and their responsibilities. This process takes a long time because they are high on solvents and often do not understand what is happening around them. One staff member sleeps on each floor at night. The children set the rules themselves, deciding what it takes to run a peaceful, equitable home. They have sessions to teach them the importance of punctuality, of equality and of good nutrition. A balance is struck between their own autonomy and what their caregivers think is beneficial for them. This training helps them to make good choices, which is practice for being part of a household when they are older.

Profile...

Jiten (17)

"I am so happy here, HOPE helped me so much".

Jiten was born in a rural area in Jharkhand. He says that his mother was a good person: "she loved me very, very much". His father was a violent alcoholic who beat his wife and children: "he hated me always". They are both dead now. He has three brothers and two sisters. Being beaten made him run away from home at the age of seven. He hopped on a train and ended up at Howrah station. He lived on the platform there for six months - "I was so starving" - until a stranger took him to a hostel for boys. They were tough on him - "so, so hard rules, I did some wrong and they hit me with a long stick for a full five minutes". He nevertheless lived there for seven years, and attended some school during this time, but kept falling behind, leaving and starting in new schools. Part of the problem was that the schools taught in Hindi and his language was

Bengali. At fourteen, he ran away from the hostel and went back to Howrah station. He met a friend there whom he had known in the hostel. This other boy took care of him and fed him. He remembers him fondly, but he was also the one to introduce him to drugs, mainly glue and hash. He went to the HOPE drop-in centre and ended up living here in Punorjibon, since August 2006. He serves as a peer educator for the boys at the drop-in centre now. He says to them about drugs "forget about them and do a good thing for your life". Sometimes they say to him "I want to be like you". He went back to his village recently and brought his little sister of eight to live here at Kasba Girl's Home. He wants to finish school and get a job, so that he can take care of his little sister when he gets older. He likes to work out at the gym and play football and cricket. He says, "I now know what is right and what is wrong". He is a young man with a strong moral compass, a survivor of a very hard life. At the ripe old age of 17, he calls the phases "my first life", "my second life" and he is now starting his "third life" as an adult.

Protection Home for the Girl Children of the Sex Workers of Kalighat Red Light Area

This project, run by Paschim Banga Krira – O – Janakalyan Parishad (PBKOJP), aims to improve the quality of life for children of commercial sex workers who work in the red light areas of Kalighat. The purpose of this project is to provide a safe and secure environment for girls who are at risk of being forced into prostitution. Its overall objective is to mainstream high-risk girls of Kalighat red light area for a better future. The Home currently has 17 girls from 7-13 years old staying in their short stay home. Girls have access to crafts, painting and dance lessons to make best use of their talents. They are given a quality education, as they need to be eligible for the job market. The Director is adamant that they do not want them to revert to their mothers' profession after all the education.

PBKOJP Building

Dipak Biswas is the Director of PBKOJP and was a founder member of this NGO in 1988. He is a former cricket player and the initial idea was to provide sports and games training in rural areas. From 1997, he was involved in rural development in Bihar. From 1999, he became involved in work in urban areas. He has been with HOPE from the start. They employ 53 staff. The run the following services:

Dipak Biswas, Director, PBKOJP

1. In 2002, they developed a vocational training centre to combat children dropping out of school and to give them an income. It is supported by the Irish Embassy. This developed into a production unit, producing marketable, good quality football and cricket jerseys. 45 girls are in vocational training, and 12 girls and women are now employed in the small production unit, using high quality sewing machines. They are paid Rs. 750-1000 a month

2. Three education centres, two crèches (20 children in each), also evening coaching sessions in each centre, helping a total of 221 boys and girls

3. A protection home for seventeen girls – all girl children of sex workers

4. A cricket coaching centre

5. Rural projects in the Sundarbans

6. Primary healthcare clinics and education and HIV awareness camps in Kalighat.

interview...

Luna

PBKOJP social worker in Kalighat

"When you see them happy, you're happy"
"We're giving them a chance to build their own lives"

Luna, PBKOJP social worker

Luna is a fount of knowledge. This warm-hearted and highly intelligent young woman knows these areas like the back of her own hand. She works on the health and education project in Kalighat, near the famous shrine to the goddess Kali. It is one of the areas men visit to gain access to prostitutes, or to use the preferred term, sex workers. One has to be sensitive to the details of local life. She says that each area is quite different: "you have to understand the community. We work in three different areas and each community has its own special character". When I ask if she is referring to the dominant religion, she says that no, whether they are Muslim or Hindu is not really the most important thing. She adds, "we have a blending of cultures in the slums, Muslims will practice the 'pujas' (rituals during Hindu religious festivals) along with their Hindu neighbours".

The women of Kalighat get into the sex trade in various ways. It is common, for example, that when a woman's husband dies, she gets thrown out of the joint (extended) family. She has to do what she can, with no other means of supporting herself and her children. She might start out doing domestic work, but since this type of work might earn her only Rs. 300 a month, that would not be enough to survive. In such straitened circumstances, she might then be driven to give sex work a try. Many years later, once established in the trade and when she gets older, she might then pimp out younger girls, maybe their own daughters. They might also marry off their own daughters, who then start having babies from a very young age.

Some girls are of course trafficked from rural areas of West Bengal or from Bangladesh. They are brought to Kalighat and 'initiated' by their handlers for maybe one year. During this 'initiation', they can be hurt or tortured as well. Many of these girls have cuts on their forearms as a kind of mark or brand. Luna says that she sometimes spots these marks on strangers' arms. These girls are very vulnerable and exposed to huge health hazards, including of course HIV/AIDS.

Interestingly, she says that the sex workers are very powerful within the domain of their own homes because they are the main earners. Men pay Rs. 20 for sex with an older woman and up to Rs.100 for sex with a teenager. Earning this relatively good income means that they have more say in decision-making compared to their 'babus', or temporary husbands. A lot of the time, these men will have left their first families and the sex workers' incomes will support them as well. So they are exploited by every man they meet. It doesn't stop them looking for love,

PBKOJP sewing production unit

though, as they want "mental protection", someone of their own. Sometimes they will use condoms with customers, but not with the babu and then pick up diseases from him. The abuse of liquor, especially among the men, is a big problem. It can occur with some women too, especially among the pavement-dwellers, who have such hard lives. In the red-light area, the sex workers would be expected to provide liquor for customers. They might have 4-5 customers per day normally, or up to 10 a day during festivals. There is no brothel system in Kalighat, but certain houses might rent out rooms to sex workers, where they have to pay Rs. 20-30 per hour.

PBKOJP runs an integrated programme within the slums with several different aspects. They run general clinics in Kalighat, but many clients will fill in CSW (Commercial Sex Worker) on their forms as their occupation. Of course, they treat everyone who comes to the clinics, not just CSWs, but they present particular issues that have to be addressed. They firstly advise them on sexual health and hygiene. They give out free condoms (which they test regularly to ensure good quality) and will accompany HIV+ patients to hospital, giving them emotional support when they need it. They give them monthly blood tests and liase with the doctor. They might intervene with the health services for them and try to give them the confidence to seek the help they need. ART (Anti Retro Viral Therapy) is free from the state, but they might be slow in going to actually seek it. She says that there is still enormous denial around AIDS. When someone dies of AIDS, it is common that their family will claim that they died of TB or cancer. They also run Hepatitis B immunisation camps in the slums. In these areas, even something very small can make a big difference. For example, HOPE refurbished toilets in the middle of Kalighat and pay a cleaner to maintain them, in an attempt to try to improve hygiene in the slum.

HOPE funds the PBKOJP coaching centre in Kalighat. This project caters for 70 children of sex workers. They have to run coaching sessions in batches of 1-2 hours because of the space restrictions. It operates in just two small rooms right in the middle of the slum. The project also attempts sex education with the girls and women, educating them on safe sex, distributing free condoms and the morning-after pill in cases of emergency. Sometimes they will encounter bias against these children in government schools. They will intervene in these schools and try to form a rapport with teachers and principals so that they will get them to take them in. They hold 'enrolment camps' in the slums, encouraging kids to go to school.

PBKOJP adopt a completely non-judgemental attitude, treating the sex workers with respect and dealing with their practical problems. They have four CHVs among them. She adds that the PBKOJP staff themselves provide role models to the young girls with whom they work. They recently staged a drama and one girl acted as a social worker, adopting Luna's own mannerisms. A tear comes to her eye as she tells me this story.

Protection Home for Vulnerable Girls in Howrah

Urban and rural poverty, disrupted and disintegrated families, accumulated family debts passed from one generation to the next, the lack of educational facilities, school dropouts, ineffective government policies and many other reasons make youngsters become children of the streets. They are dispersed throughout urban centres and the inhuman reality of their lives remains mostly hidden and ignored. Girls are the worst victims of this situation. SEED runs a protection home for such girl children. These are girls who were found living in and around the high-risk zone of Howrah station. 36 girls are supported by this Home. At present, 20 girls are living in the home and 14 girls are attending boarding school. Each of these children will be provided with shelter, nutrition, clothing, education, counselling and healthcare in a caring and secure environment.

Shelter Home for HIV Infected and Affected Children

HOPE funds **Snehneer,** the shelter home run by Bhoruka Public Welfare Trust (BPWT) for up to 25 HIV/AIDS infected and affected children. By this is meant that either the children themselves or their parents are HIV+. They take care of all their needs – health, educational, nutritional, psychological and recreational. The children are provided with holistic care and support, receiving nutritious meals and all the health care facilities they need. They get them enrolled into government schools too, even though they sometimes encounter bias and discriminatory attitudes. The aim of this project is to create an enabling environment in society by ensuring the basic rights of children infected and affected by HIV/AIDS.

They also try to change public consciousness on AIDS. They reject use of the word 'AIDS victim', using the term 'People Living With HIV/AIDS' (PLWHA) instead. They work to combat stigma against those with HIV. Often nobody wants to touch a HIV+ child or play with them, but they have to be rehabilitated within their community. Dr. Mishra from BPWT says that the woman is often blamed for her husband going "outside", i.e. having sex with someone else. Their focus is on children. As Dr. Mishra says, "these children have not committed a sin".

P.D. Agarwal, the founder of the Transport Corporation of India was behind the creation of the Bhoruka Blood Bank in 1982, formed to improve blood banking services in Eastern India and to treat blood disorders like thalassaemia and haemophilia. He wanted to ensure the availability and accessibility of safe and quality blood for all. It was especially important to discourage professional blood donors and promote only voluntary blood donation. At Bhoruka, a team of qualified, efficient and dedicated technicians are working round the clock to provide blood and blood components to patients requiring transfusions. Since 1988, there has been routine HIV testing of donations, and since 1998, they have been screening for Hepatitis C. They also organise voluntary blood donation camps in Kolkata and suburbs. They work on HIV/AIDS, trafficking, reproductive health and child health.

Bhoruka Public Welfare Trust

Other services they provide are:

- They have a programme in the Khiddirpur area of the city, providing education, vocational training and economic empowerment for Muslim girls there

- Targeted intervention project:
  Bhoruka has taken the initiative from the very beginning of intervening to control HIV infection, targeting truckers and sex workers at different ports and truck halting spots. They have camps that try to prevent risky behaviour, using banners, radio ads, informal discussions and films, street plays and games. They also hold mobile clinics on STIs and HIV, where they have counselling, give out condoms and prescribe medications. They also try to make sure condoms are as widely available as possible

- They also target female sex workers in Guwahati in Assam, where they provide medical and psychological help and form self-help groups among the women

- They have Community Care Centres (CCCs) in rural areas where people living with HIV/AIDS can get their ART (antiretroviral therapy), drugs, food, counselling and advice

- They also set up vigilance committees in rural areas, especially around the border with Bangladesh and Nepal against trafficking.

- HOPE funds a Child Watch programme against child labour, begging and drug abuse

- HOPE funds a Holistic education project for 35 children, looking after all of their needs

Bhoruka have branches throughout N.E. India, providing vital services in:
Assam, Darjeeling, W. Bengal, Andhra Pradesh, Orissa, Bihar.

Protection Home for Women/Girls, Victims of Trafficking and Other Forms of Violence In Kolkata

"Due to the curse of poverty and illiteracy, trafficking is increasing more and more"

(HRLN Annual Report, 2008/9).

This is a Protection Home for victims of trafficking and other forms of violence in Kolkata. The project, run by HRLN and funded by HOPE, provides temporary shelter to women and young girls who have been victims of this type of abuse, or who are in danger of becoming victims. There are twelve girls there at present. In the protection home they are also prepared for return to their families if possible, and in other cases help them stand on their own feet. The project deals with needy women in general as well as trafficked women and girls in the course of its regular jail and court work.

Such women and girls are always in need of shelter as, having been rescued from traffickers and other perpetrators of violence, they face tremendous personal stress and trauma. These women are provided with shelter in the interim period. With this help, these women and girls are saved from being repeat victims of trafficking and other forms of violence. Some of these women also require legal aid in their ongoing battles against perpetrators, and through free legal aid, these cases are supported along with the provision of temporary accommodation. The project provides shelter, food, medical care, psychological counselling, vocational training, legal aid/legal counselling and either formal or informal education as required. HRLN submit Quarterly Reports to HOPE, including psychological and medical reports from the doctor and counsellor.

interview...

Sutapa Chakraborty
Secretary, HRLN Kolkata

Mrs. Chakraborty has had a long legal career, having worked on human rights issues all of her life. She is a legal rights advisor and former Special Officer of Calcutta High Court. Mrs. Chakraborty also functions as a judge in the local people's court, where differences are settled with minimum fuss and cost. They employ the services of some lawyers who give their services free of charge. When she worked in the High Court, she came across prisoners labelled 'non-criminal lunatics' who were "languishing" in prison because there was nowhere else to put them. Also, there were women and girls in there "in the name of safe keeping". She worked to improve conditions for them there. Through this work, she saw the need to set up a shelter home especially for trafficked girls.

There is little that she does not know about the issue of trafficking. Touts pay bribes to parents to get their daughters a job or a husband. Many thousands of girls and women go missing and no one knows where they end up. HRLN try to train the village and slum-dwelling poor to spot the methods used by the touts. It is a difficult issue because the girls are often sold by their own relatives.

She organises legal awareness camps in urban slums and in rural villages to make people aware of their rights, especially 'BPL' people, those officially living below the poverty line. The themes of these camps have included 'Food Security and Livelihood of the BPL Group', that advised the poor on how to access rations to which they are entitled. Another was 'To Combat Trafficking and the Protection of the Girl Child'. Another camp was on 'The Prevention of Domestic Violence Against Women'. They mediate in families and seek to resolve differences. Another camp was on the rights of disabled people, who are often unaware of their rights. Another was on 'Muslim Personal Law'. She says, "'talaq' is the curse of that society". This is when a Muslim man can obtain a legal divorce simply by saying the words "I divorce you" three times. The only means of empowerment is education. Another camp on 'Women and the Law' was augmented by a session with role-playing, story telling and a quiz. These methods of course help to reach those who may be illiterate.

This woman is a highly respected figure in the community. She is a strong person who has a lot of experience in the field of human rights. She is thus a great ally with whom HOPE can work, in order to reach out to trafficked women and girls, some of the most exploited people on the face of this earth.

HOPE PARTNER: HUMAN RIGHTS LAW NETWORK (HRLN)

The HRLN is a collective of lawyers and social activists dedicated to the use of the legal system to advance human rights, struggle against violations, and ensure access to justice for all. A not-for-profit NGO, HRLN defines rights to include civil and political rights as well as economic, social, cultural and environmental rights. They believe human rights are universal and indivisible.

Starting in 1989 as an informal group of lawyers and social activists, HRLN has evolved into a human rights organisation with an active presence in many states of India. It provides *pro bono* legal services to those with little or no access to the justice system. It participates in the struggle for rights through its various activities including public interest litigation, advocacy, legal awareness programmes, investigations into violations, publishing 'know yours rights' materials, and participating in campaigns. It collaborates with social movements and grassroots development groups to enforce the rights of children, Dalits, disabled people, farmers, HIV+ people, the homeless, indigenous peoples, prisoners, refugees, religious and sexual minorities, women, and workers, among others. They use the legal system to participate in various struggles for human rights.

HRLN Goals:
- To create a justice delivery system that is accessible, accountable, transparent, efficient and affordable, and works for the underprivileged.
- To protect fundamental human rights, increase access to basic resources for marginalized communities and to eliminate all forms of discrimination.
- To raise the level of *pro bono* legal expertise for the poor to make the work uniformly competent as well as compassionate.
- To equip through professional training a new generation of public interest lawyers and para-legals

who are comfortable both in the world of law as well as in social movements, and who learn from the social movements to refine legal concepts and strategies.

- To work towards an increased awareness of rights as universal and indivisible, and their realisation as an immediate goal.
- To work to increase women's access to the justice system, as a vital means of empowerment. They provide comprehensive free legal services to poor and marginalized women concerned about such issues as sexual assault, domestic violence, sexual harassment in the workplace, matrimonial cruelty and disputes, reproductive and sexual health rights of women/adolescent girls, pre-birth sex-selection and elimination of female foetuses and trafficking for commercial sexual exploitation.

All Bengal Women's Union (ABWU) Midway Home for Girls

The overall aim of the Midway Home Project is to overcome the problems arising out of the admission of disturbed and traumatised children to the ABWU Children's Welfare Home by providing intensive counselling support, enabling them to adjust to the home with greater ease. The children remain at the Midway Home for varying lengths of time, depending on each individual's needs, but usually for 3-6 months. Two dormitories at the home accommodate 10 girls each. Two counsellors provide counselling and psychological support. These children are entitled to join the dance and work therapies as well as extra-curricular activities and also to participate in all the excursions and competitions available to the rest of the girls. As well as the Midway Home, HOPE funds:

- Sponsorship of 30 children
- Counsellors for all their children
- The crèche
- Child protection team, who implement child protection policy within homes and also do outreach work on domestic child labour.

interview...

Amita Sen
Hon. General Secretary, All Bengal Women's Union (ABWU)

Amita Sen, Secretary, ABWU

"It's feminism without all the hullabaloo"

"Women are being treated as property, almost like cattle - first the property of the father, then of the husband, then later on, the son"

"Each child has her own story – no two can be compared"

Ms. Sen is the Chairperson of the Child Welfare Committee. This results from the Juvenile Justice (for Care and Protection of Children) Act, 2000. Under this, children are divided into two categories. These are firstly "children in conflict with the law" and secondly "children in need of care and protection". This led to the instigation of the Juvenile Justice Board and the Child Welfare Committee. She finds her work on this committee "heart-rending" and gets tearful at the thought of some of the cases she sees. She tells the story of one little girl who told her "with a stone face" how

Weaving workshop at ABWU

she saw her father stab her mother to death in front of her.

They also do legal outreach work free of charge, where they go out into the villages with a legal team, a judge and lawyers, and set up a local people's court to resolve legal problems and bring justice. They use these forums for education too, giving lectures on domestic violence, trafficking and women's rights. Also, three lawyers give free legal advice to women every Saturday at their city centre premises.

Trafficking is the issue that exercises her most. ABWU set up legal camps in rural villages training people on how to be vigilant against those who want to steal their children. The reasons she sees as to why trafficking is so common are "economic reasons, large families, and ignorance". They are often fooled by "would-be grooms who flaunt their wealth" and who say they want to marry their daughters. They might be offered work in the city too, maybe by touts or go-betweens who promise to take care of them. They say, "if she is not married, how can we keep her safe?" If she is married off, she is no longer their responsibility, as she 'belongs' to her husband. This encourages marriage at 14 or 15, to protect the girl's virginity. She reports that when they rescue girls from Bangladesh, they have to go through huge legal wrangles to get girls accepted back over the border - every blockage is put in their way.

She is passionate about women's economic empowerment, building self-reliance and self-confidence. She says that if a woman in a family puts her foot down, she will not allow her child to be trafficked, sold, married young, or made to work as a child. The only thing that increases women's say in the family is earning more money. She advocates the development of Self-Help Groups (SHGs), micro-credit organisations and co-op banks, which are now evident throughout West Bengal.

In spite of the existence of rampant trafficking of women and children in West Bengal, there is very limited focused intervention on combating the issue. Joining the fight against trafficking, the Hope Foundation has formed partnerships with organisations committed to the rescue and rehabilitation of victims, aiding their reintegration into society. Through community awareness campaigns they endeavour to mobilise society to stamp out this illegal trade in human misfortune.

Spotlight 5: Child Trafficking

The trafficking of women and children is one of the most distressing realities in the modern world. It is currently the third largest illegal trade in existence, behind drug smuggling and gun running. Human trafficking is estimated by the United Nations to generate $7 billion every year.[8] Child trafficking is a particular problem. It is thought to be of a magnitude ten times larger than the trans-Atlantic slave trade was at its peak in the late 18th century.[9] It is difficult to draw a dividing line between the issues of child labour, trafficking, bonded labour, gender discrimination, prostitution and slavery. They all intersect in mind-boggling ways and are closely linked by poverty, powerlessness and misogyny. The horrors that are foisted upon millions of Indian children do not belong in any country that calls itself a democracy.

India is indeed a major centre of human trafficking, the majority of which is within the country itself, and some over its borders to the north. The National Human Rights Commission estimates that every year, 44,500 children go missing, of which 11,000 are never traced. The majority are in forced adoptions or marriages, but they are also used for child labour, the entertainment industry and sex tourism.[10] It is a very complex problem, as it takes many forms. Sometimes children are simply stolen, sometimes they are actually sold to agents by their parents, but most often poor women and children are tricked by traffickers into thinking a better life awaits them in employment or in marriage. Although hardly a new phenomenon, trafficking has taken on alarming forms and proportions in India over the past decade.

Child trafficking is defined as the recruitment, transportation, transfer, harbouring or receipt of a child for the purpose of exploitation, within or outside a country, including (but not limited to) sexual exploitation, child labour, services, slavery, servitude, removal and sale of organs, use in illicit/ illegal activities and participation in armed conflict. It also includes the recruitment, transportation, transfer, harbouring or receipt of a child by means of adoption or marriage for the purpose of exploitation.

As West Bengal shares international borders with Bangladesh, Bhutan and Nepal, it occupies a key position on the international trafficking route. UNICEF argue that there is "weak law enforcement and inefficient and corrupt policing of the borders" in this area.[11] Studying the social context is all-important. West Bengal is a very poor state, as are surrounding states like Orissa, Jharkhand and Bihar. These states have among the highest rates of poverty, illiteracy and unemployment in the whole country. This part of the world is inhabited by people for whom caste discrimination, hunger, malnutrition and indebtedness are normal parts of life. Severe gender discrimination means that girls are seen as nothing more than a financial burden.

Predators lurk within children's own communities and sometimes even their own families. People are desperately poor and the lives of children, especially girls, are cheap. There are usually large families with too many mouths to feed because women have been subjugated all their lives, viewed as nothing more than child bearers and domestic labourers. Female illiteracy is very high in this area, which increases their vulnerability when dealing with traffickers. They easily believe the stories that the traffickers spin about the opportunities that await them in the cities. Their lives are often so unrelentingly hard that they would believe anyone who told them they would get them a job in an exciting big city.

These socio-economic factors, along with weak regulatory measures and uncertain policing, have lead to burgeoning human trafficking across these borders, particularly in women and children. Kolkata is a source, a transit point and a destination for trafficked children and women, with the huge train stations of Howrah and Sealdah being notorious hubs for the movement of this human cargo. These vulnerable people are kidnapped, sold or duped by traffickers with promises of marriage or employment.

They frequently end up being sexually exploited in brothels in red-light districts across India. There are estimated to be about three million prostitutes in India. Of these, 40 per cent are children, so the child prostitute population is close to 1.2 million. At least 100 million people are involved in human trafficking in India, so it is a major illicit industry.[12] Local activists estimate that as many as 30,000 children, mostly girls, are trafficked into Kolkata every year for use in the sex trade. With so much male migration into such cities, there is a growing demand for commercial sex. There is also increasing demand for younger girls as there is a belief that sex with young girls can cure men of STDs or HIV, as well as the perception that there is less chance of catching a disease from a new, fresh, recent arrival to the prostitution scene. These vulnerable girls are so readily available in this poor, highly populated region that "after she becomes old or ill, or is infected with HIV/AIDS, the trafficker abandons her. He no longer arranges for her bail or pays the fine for her pleading guilty, and she is left alone to face trial and the due process of the law".[13] These are disposable people and there are plenty more to replace them to make more profits for those who exploit them so unscrupulously.

UNICEF reports that children are trafficked for these other types of work as well as sex work. These are:
- Forced labour in the carpet and textile industries
- Forced or bonded domestic work where children can be treated like slaves
- Forced labour in construction sites
- Forced employment in bars, massage parlours and other forms of entertainment
- Begging
- The illicit trade in bodily organs, notably kidneys
- Forced and illegal marriages
- Camel jockeying, where children are often hurt or killed
- Buying and selling babies for illegal adoptions, in India and abroad.[14]

It is not an exaggeration to redefine trafficking as the modern slave trade. In fact, in many ways, the contemporary form is much worse than the older one. Kevin Bales, an expert on slavery, outlines the differences between the old and new forms. In 1850 in the American South, an average slave sold for what was the equivalent of about $75,000. This was a huge investment, as the slave was legally owned by the slaveholder. Slaves and their children were therefore viewed as valuable assets, commodities that had to be taken care of, to some extent, even if they were sick or old. Today, slavery is illegal everywhere so one human being cannot be legally owned by another anywhere in the world. Today's slaves are cheap and disposable.[15] Eastern Europe is a major source area for girls to be exploited in the sex trade. One researcher found that "any bar owner in Greece can send someone up to southern Bulgaria to buy women for cash. The cost of a girl in that area is $1,000, or, if you negotiate, you might be able to get two for $1,000. Best to try on a Monday for cheap prices, because most trafficking happens at weekends. Mondays are slow, so you can get the leftovers".[16] In India, the price of a girl is much, much lower – perhaps as low as $30. There is a glut of poor vulnerable people here and in other parts of the developing world, so they can easily be replaced and/or moved to the places where they can generate the most profit for the slaveholders. They can be abandoned or even killed when they are no longer productive, or as would be common in the sex industry, when they develop HIV/AIDS.

This injustice is exacerbated further by the fact that the biggest proportion of slaves are those who are in debt bondage. This was also referred to in Spotlight 4 on child labour. This is where "a person pledges him- or herself against a loan of money, but the length and nature of the service are not defined and the labour does not reduce the original debt. The debt can be passed down to subsequent generations, thus enslaving offspring; moreover, "defaulting" can be punished by seizing and selling children into further debt bonds".[17] These contemporary slaves suffer major human rights violations, as they are denied their liberty and humane working conditions, and are routinely subjected to gross exploitation, violence and sexual abuse.

There is very slow progress on this issue in India, as those in power have a very ambivalent attitude towards it. For example, the middle class and the rich benefit from having ready access to vulnerable and readily exploitable children to work in their homes. The conditions under which domestic workers toil are often deplorably cruel. Also, the deeply hierarchical nature of Indian society means that the poor are often seen as almost sub-human by their employers. The exploitation that they mete out is seen as appropriate, 'natural' and part of the established order where low castes are meant to serve the higher ones. No doubt, such underlying issues will not be eliminated from Indian society any time soon. However, the sterling work done by NGOs like HOPE and its partners on this issue can only help to force the subject into the public domain and ultimately contribute to positive change in this regard.

"Traffickers are always looking for fresh faces, as prostitution thrives on age, looks, physical form, virgin status and bearing. Procurers scout for girls in villages and urban slums in order to identify persons/households, mainly impoverished, illiterate and indebted, with a large number of dependents and hardly any earning member. Problem households where husbands are alcoholic, unemployed, or harshly treat their children and abuse them, fall into this list. Once such families have been located, information about them is passed on to persons who arrive on the scene posing as recruiting agents for girls to be employed in cities or towns. These agents give a hefty advance to the family, which they find hard to resist, and assure the family that remittances will continue to flow as the girls start work.

Once out of the village, the girls are often sexually abused by the procurers themselves, unless the intention is to sell her off as a virgin who would secure a much higher price. Procurers keep the girls in custody and brutalise them if they dare to disobey. The traffickers know the agents and the cities where prices are negotiated. They are then sold and resold at different points of the network and finally land at the brothel.

Fake marriages are yet another device adopted to take the girl away from the village. Girls who are maltreated in their homes are lured by scouting agents who promise them an escape from the harsh circumstances of their home to become self-employed in cities/towns where they have contacts. Once the girl is out of the village or slum, there is no means of escape as she is inexperienced, illiterate or semi-literate, without money, and no knowledge of whom to approach.

Some girls, usually 10-14 years of age, are procured by agents from backward districts on payment, often as low as Rs. 2,000, to very poor families, on the pretext of marriage to a farmer in Punjab, Haryana, or some other state where there is a shortage of girls of marriageable age. Parents give away the girl as there is little value attached to her, there would be one less mouth to feed, and dowry expenses would be spared.

The demand is growing for young, pre-pubescent girls, as there is a common belief that sex with these children cures STDs and HIV. Between 1994 and 2000, only 110 people were charged with procuring minor girls each year. Incompetence, corruption and possibly police collusion slows down and hampers the legal process".

A.B.Bose, 2006 'Child Development in India' in *India: Social Development Report*

HOPE PARTNER: HALDERCHAWK CHETANA WELFARE SOCIETY (HCWS)

Halderchawk Chetana Welfare Society (HCWS), a HOPE partner, is committed to the rescue, rehabilitation, reintegration and repatriation of trafficked persons through community interaction and awareness raising and policy level intervention. They are based in a quiet village in the delta area of the Sundarbans near Kolkata. It exists since July 2006, and is funded by HOPE, GOAL India, WWF (Netherlands) and Caritas India. It's co-ordinator is Narayan Duraya. This village is in a rice growing area, which is harvested June to October. To grow anything else, irrigation is a big problem and expense. Incomes are very low. Most families own no land and work as day labourers during harvest time for local landowners. Apart from that, they migrate all over India for work. Some are fishermen but they only fish for half the year as well. So families are very poor here and it can be very easy for traffickers to convince women and girls to move to other areas for marriage or work, to escape the poverty and drudgery of the village.

Narayan Duraya. Co-ordinator, HCWS

The stories of trafficking are very varied. Those involved can be relatives, neighbours or strangers. There is a source area, a transit area and a target area. There is a chain of command and the first person to meet the girl is usually a woman, as it is easier to establish trust. HCWS run awareness campaigns, making people aware that anyone can be a trafficker, even the girl's father or stepmother. They go around to schools to talk to young people, and they find that some schools are more co-operative than others. They provide training for local community volunteers to empower them so that HCWS can then move on to more needy villages, where traffickers have an easier time. This trade spreads its tentacles throughout communities. It has significant parallels with the drug trade, because the money is so tempting for very poor people. They can earn up to Rs.100,000 (c. €1,470) for a girl, a small fortune in India.

Many rescued persons suffer from depression, have abused drugs, or suffer from STDs or HIV/AIDS. Therefore psychosocial counselling is important for them. Because the girls are often stigmatised in the socially conservative villages they come from, their social re-integration can be difficult. Efforts are made to reunite the victims with their families over time.

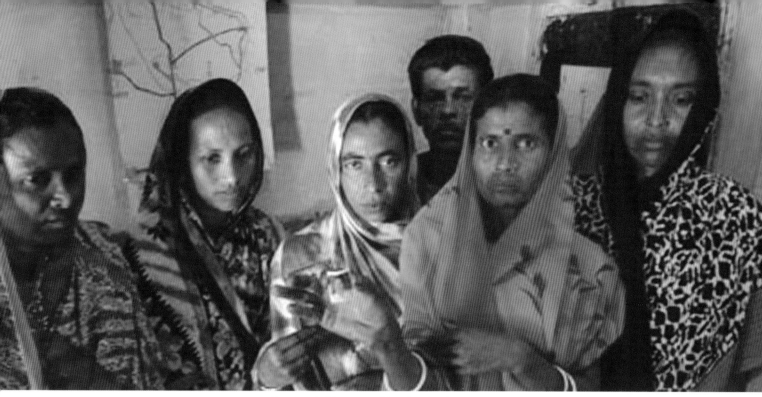

A group of mothers hold pictures of their lost daughters [Provision]

Grandfather of a rescued girl

Two mothers of trafficked girls who are still missing

Rescued!

'Amita', 19 years, is a local girl from the Sundarbans. She dropped out of school in Class 7, at the age of fifteen. One day in June 2009, on the way to visiting an aunt, she met a woman at a train station who befriended her and bought her food. The food was evidently drugged and she was brought to Howrah station, from where she was brought to Pune. This is a 36-hour train trip, but she can only barely remember it, as she was drugged and drowsy. She was kept like that for two days after her arrival. She was locked in a room in a red-light area. She was kept there for five months, during which time she was tortured and forced to have sex with three or four men a day. She never saw any money as it was given directly to the brothel keeper. Eventually, a man came as a customer who spoke Bengali. He took pity on her and she gave him a contact number at home. The police were told and they got in touch with HCWS, and they went and rescued her. The family are too afraid to pursue it in court and the culprit has got away scot-free. This girl is well supported by her parents, who accompanied her to this interview. She is one of eight children. Her mother recently had an operation for a brain tumour that cost Rs. 80,000, so they can't afford to do without the girl's labour at home. This means that she cannot go back to school. Not every problem can be easily solved…

Simple life in the village of Halderchawk in the Sundarbans. Rice is the main crop grown here. Incomes are very low, which makes it easy for traffickers to ply their trade.

Rescued

'**Rani**' was stolen at 12, and she is now 14. She was in a dance group with six other girls. They were kidnapped and brought to Bihar. They were worked hard, forced to perform their dance very frequently. One of the girls insisted she needed to see a doctor and she escaped to call home. The local police initially didn't do anything. The local people raised part of the money themselves and HCWS raised the rest. This was a racket run by a mafia group in Bihar. They suspected that the police there were in on it too. Eventually the West Bengal police and the NGO and locals set up a posse to go save the girls. They were kept locked up in a room like a cage, even with railings in the ceiling. They were away 18 days. They were too young for the sex trade, but were threatened with being sent to brothels if they didn't obey. Her grandfather is very grateful to HCWS for bringing her home.

'**Sunita**' was rescued after 2 years. She had been trafficked by her husband, who was migrant labourer from Bihar. He was an alcoholic in a lot of debt, so he needed money. He pimped out his wife for sex and then sold her to other Biharis. A neighbour smuggled the girl out and traced her family. She was then rescued by HCWS. She is now happy and working as a domestic worker in a house in Kolkata.

Rescued

Yet to be rescued

'**Lakshmi**', a girl of 18, has been trafficked. She was married with one son. She was unhappy in her marriage, tortured by in-laws regularly because she couldn't afford the Rs. 10,000 dowry they demanded. They kept her prisoner and she was suicidal. She was nabbed by strangers and kidnapped. Another girl who was taken at the same time has since returned, so they know that she was sold into marriage to an elderly Muslim man in Kashmir. So he now has a wife and a slave. Her mother got upset when telling the story, especially because the girl's son has to grow up without her and because the food habits there are totally different. They also acknowledge that she might be better off where she is, because she left such an unhappy situation. The other girl now doesn't want to get involved with the case because her family are also probably involved in the trade. HCWS went all the way to Kashmir and spent a week searching houses for her, but did not succeed in finding her. The case is ongoing.

[1] John & Narayanan, 2006: 190.
[2] Human Rights Watch, 1996.
[3] Luce, 2006: 330.
[4] Human Rights Watch, 2003.
[5] John & Narayanan, 2006: 181.
[6] Ibid: 188.
[7] Luce, 2006: 332.
[8] UNICEF, 2006: 2.
[9] McMichael, 2008:207.
[10] O'Connell, 2007.
[11] UNICEF, 2006: 2.
[12] *Times of India* Dec 14th, 2009.
[13] UNICEF, 2006: 3.
[14] UNICEF, 2006:4.
[15] Bales, 2000: 14-19.
[16] Cockburn, 2003: 10.
[17] Bales, 2000: 20.

gender

Poverty and unemployment are major problems in India, as in other underdeveloped countries. Official estimates of poverty always underestimate the real extent of deprivation that actually exists. The challenge of gathering reliable data in such an enormous country with such a huge illiterate population means that these figures are virtually meaningless. As explained in earlier parts of this book, the creation of new employment is too low to match the huge number of new entrants to the job market every year. This is without taking into account the challenge of clearing the backlog. This means that employment creation schemes need to be a priority for an NGO like HOPE, who are trying to improve the lot of the poor. One certainty is that the vast majority of Indian workers are employed in the informal economy, and therefore have no social security. It is to this important aspect of the economy that we now turn.

4 Gender
skill development & income generation projects

PROJECT	NAME OF PARTNER NGOS
Empowering Marginalized Underprivileged Women through Self Help Group, Micro Credit, Vocational Training and Income Generation	HKF, PBKOJP, MJCC
Skill Development Project	PBKOJP, ABWU

Spotlight 6: The Informal Economy in India

When we think about work in the Western world, we make a straight distinction between employment and unemployment. The unemployed are easily counted because they receive social welfare, monies that are set aside by the state for those who are less fortunate. They are therefore on the Unemployment Register.

However, in poorer countries like India, things are not so black and white. Poorer people have to do what they can to survive, in the absence of a generous welfare state. This also renders reliable statistics virtually impossible to gather. There are many, many different types of work that are obscured, rather than revealed, by statistics. Most people work in what is sometimes pejoratively called the black economy, that which in India is dubbed the unorganised sector, but is most commonly termed the informal economy.

Working on Kolkata's streets in the informal sector.

The informal economy is a broad, inclusive term that includes types of jobs that are legal and illegal, badly paid and well paid. It encompasses petty trading - like selling cigarettes or chewing gum on the streets, shoe shining, windscreen cleaning or busking, self-employment, casual and irregular waged work, jobs in personal services or in small-scale businesses. Prostitution and drug dealing could be included in this sector as well. Those unable to find regular wage employment swell the ranks of this sector, because one can drift in and out easily enough, without much education or personal or financial investment.

This is different to the formal, or organised, economy, usually providing relatively stable employment, higher wages and better working conditions. Workers can also represent themselves in unions in this economy. It is estimated that only seven per cent of workers, that is only 35 million out of 470 million, enjoy the relative stability of the formal economy and contribute income tax to state coffers. Of this, 21 million work for the state and only 14 million are in the private sector. The much-lauded IT sector has as yet only yielded about one million jobs. One of the major reasons that this figure is so low is that part of Nehru's legacy is one of the strictest sets of labour laws in the world. This

means that it is nearly impossible to fire a worker no matter how they perform. This means that industrialists see outsourcing to the unregulated unorganised sector as their best option.[1] The well-meaning state, it seems, has cut off its nose to spite its face.

Another important reason that this reserve army of labour exists on the streets of Indian cities and throughout the developing world is the mass migration of people from the countryside to the cities. There are many problems in rural India that drive people into the cities to try to make better lives for themselves and their families. The biggest of these is of course terrible poverty, where lots of people are undernourished, not even getting to eat a meal every day. Millions of farmers suffer intolerable levels of debt and suicide levels are inordinately high in rural India. Services are also a problem in many areas, where roads, water supplies, hospitals and schools are poor or non-existent. People can have very few opportunities to rise out of lives of grinding poverty, and life in cities like Kolkata, however harsh, seems far more attractive to them. People think that there are more chances of getting work and earning higher incomes, and they have access to more social services. Many millions of these migrants end up living on the streets and in slums, but this is still seen as preferable to the isolation of the countryside. The tribulations of the fictional character of Hasari Pal in Dominique Lapierre's novel *City of Joy* are an unforgettable illustration of this predicament. Real people make this same decision every day, adding to the ranks of the poor in Indian cities.

When we look closer, we see that the informal economy actually serves as a support system for the formal capitalist economy. Formal and informal economic activities are closely connected, and in fact complementary to each other. Firstly, large companies subcontract work out to smaller firms, and in this way, labour and child protection legislation can be avoided. The textiles industry often works in this way, employing cheap, unorganised, female or child labourers. This gives large companies great flexibility to experiment with different product lines. Also in this category are informal types of work like garbage picking, which reduces the need for recycling programmes, and it is also beneficial for companies that make goods like cigarettes and chewing gum to have street sellers of their goods on every corner.

Secondly, the existence of this reserve army of labour outside the doors of factories means that it can lower wages among those who have jobs inside. The workforce are held to ransom and cannot demand higher wages, as they are told that there are millions of others out there who would be only too happy to replace them if they are not happy.

Thirdly, it cheapens the cost of producing a workforce for the state and for industry. This means that when people get used to having such poor lifestyles, they can learn to survive on very little. It makes

life cheaper when people get used to very harsh lives and become less demanding.

Fourthly, when goods are sold in small local shops and street stalls, they are usually more expensive than if they were bought in bulk in a supermarket. The poor can only afford to buy a little at a time, and hence are never able to afford to bulk buy. Also, when they live on the streets or in slums, they have no space or refrigeration to store food. This is likewise true for petty traders like small builders, who can never afford to bulk buy their materials.

Women are often relegated to the worst forms of work in the informal economy, enduring low pay and terrible conditions. Typical forms of work would be sewing piecework, baking to sell at street stalls, sex work, child minding and domestic service. Most of this work is very isolated, without any social contact or sense of collective belonging, or certainly without any labour rights. Women's work is underestimated because domestic work is statistically invisible, even in the Western world.

However, the variety of types of work done by India's poor bears testimony to their entrepreneurship and creativity in extremely tough circumstances. This popular economy can be a source of co-operation and community for the women and men on society's margins. It is the very essence of people helping themselves in the face of adversity. The conditions they have to endure, however, are unspeakably difficult, and as long as people can survive like this, the state is more likely to be abdicated of its responsibilities towards these citizens.

Education for deprived urban children is a major focus for the Hope Foundation. Many children do not continue education after they reach the age of fourteen. Boys often engage themselves in informal occupations like pulling cycle vans, selling vegetables, running petty grocery shops, tea and snacks stalls, and some get involved in criminal activities. Income for this group of boys varies, but is usually around Rs. 500 a month, though many earn even less than this. Many of the girls among the poorest sectors are either married off at an early age or lured into the sex trade. Working as commercial sex workers is financially attractive for girls as they can make what is seen as substantial amounts of money by Indian standards, ranging from Rs. 1,000 to 3,000 per month. Most of these girls practice unsafe sex with multiple partners and have little knowledge about STDs or HIV/AIDS. Therefore vocational and life skills training is very necessary. This type of practical education can have a huge impact on empowering young women and men to be financially independent.

In urban areas like Kolkata, it is very important to develop the skills of the vulnerable poor and to involve them in income-generating activities. One of the most effective methods of reducing poverty and to promote gainful employment is 'Self Help Groups' (SHGs). Originally developed as part of the highly successful Grameen Bank initiative in Bangladesh in the 1970s, they were used as tools to ameliorate poverty and improve rural development. This was a small-scale savings scheme with high interest rates that was designed to encourage local entrepreneurship. It is therefore not a handout, because people have a serious stake in its success. They have since become common in poor cities all over the world. A SHG is a small group of the poor who voluntarily come together to save small amounts of money regularly. Such savings are deposited in a common fund to meet the members' emergency needs and to provide collateral-free loans, having been agreed upon by the group. The SHG system has proven to be very effective in offering women the possibility of freeing themselves from the exploitation and isolation that has been their lot for centuries. The basic principles of the SHGs are group cohesiveness, mutual trust, organisation of small manageable groups, a spirit of thrift, demand-based lending, women-friendly loans, peer group pressure for repayment, skills training, capacity building and empowerment. This initiative operates in a context of severe discrimination against women in many countries, including India.

Little girls who do not get to go to school

Spotlight 7: Gender Discrimination in India

"I do not wish women to have power over men, but over themselves"

Mary Wollstonecraft, British feminist writer (1759-1797).

If one is born female in India, it is possible to have a very privileged and charmed life. Indian women have excelled in every field imaginable, be it literature, drama, music, law, medicine, engineering or science. The possibilities are endless for those girls who are born into families who treasure them and who are in a position to provide for them and educate them as much as they wish.

There has been an active women's movement in India since the nineteenth century. As far back as the mid 19th century, a group of Calcutta middle class women initiated a reform movement that led to the banning of sati (widows' self-immolation). They also campaigned for girls' education and against child marriage. In the early twentieth century, women became involved in the nationalist movement led by Mahatma Gandhi, who believed that "woman is the companion of man, gifted with equal mental capacities", and that they could work as "comrades in common service" with their husbands.[2] After gaining independence from the British in 1947, the Constitution they drew up in 1950 was very progressive in granting equality to women, as well as providing for positive discrimination in their favour.[3] However, there have been "glaring mismatches between intent and action".[4] Indira Gandhi was a major world political figure who served four terms as Prime Minister from 1966 until her assassination in 1984. While she could not be termed a feminist, she nevertheless became a role model for other women. The Congress Party slogan in 1975 was "Indira is India, India is Indira". The activities of the Indian women's movement continue in various forms, scattered both within India itself and among the diasporic community of Non Resident Indians (NRIs) abroad. The current President of India is Pratibha Devisingh Patil, who took up her prestigious role in July 2007.

However, for the vast majority of Indian women, life is much harder than this. While positive legislation exists on paper, most are probably not aware of it, as they are illiterate, exploited and isolated in rural villages, in which about three quarters of the population live. The Indian family is the site of much of women's oppression. Conservative attitudes reign because people cannot afford to take risks with gender roles. Prasad explains, "since there is no social security in our country, the family is our social security".[5] It is common for little boys to be valued more, and hence fed and educated better than girls. The birth of a boy is seen as a blessing because the family name is passed on. Also, they are seen as an economic asset as they will bring in dowry money to the family when they marry, and they are expected to look after their parents when they get old. Daughters, on the other hand, are often seen as an economic liability because their parents will have to save for their dowries. The behaviour of girls is strictly monitored as well, as maintaining their virginity for marriage is of paramount importance.[6] One cannot help thinking that if the state provided for people in their old age as in other countries, such strict rules might not then apply, as people could feel more secure about their futures.

The first test that girls face is to be born at all in the first place. A 1997 UNICEF report found that India is "missing" 40-60 million females. Demographers have established that the "perfect" male-female ratio worldwide is 100:105. In India, it is 100:90, and in some areas as low as 100:85. Amartya Sen has conducted extensive research on this subject and has found that the problem is generally much worse in the states in the north and west of the country. Those to the east and south, including West Bengal, fare much better. The worse offenders are the states of Punjab, Haryana, Delhi and Gujarat.[7] Most of these girl babies are aborted after amniocentesis reveals their sex - a clash of modern technology and traditional attitudes. There are less girl children in urban areas because of access to that technology. Many others are killed after birth, often by poisoning, others still neglected or abused so that they die a premature death. This is confirmed by Sen, who states, "there is indeed considerable direct evidence that female children are neglected in terms of health care, hospitalisation and even feeding".[8] So because females are subject to discrimination in health care and nutrition, they are at a higher risk of not surviving past the age of five.

Most girls born to the poor have a life of little more than a beast of burden ahead of them, with no opportunities for education and advancement. An American writer, Elizabeth Bumiller, who has researched this subject, interviewed some women who had recently poisoned their baby girls.[9] One said to her "I think I have done the right thing. Why should a child suffer like me?" When one travels in India and sees first-hand the drudgery of most village women's lives, one can almost begin to understand her reasoning.

One of the main reasons for the persistence of this discrimination against the girl-child is the continued importance of dowry, even though it was outlawed in 1961 under the Dowry Prohibition Act. Social custom still dictates that on marriage, the bride's family must produce a huge amount of visible wealth in the form of gold, expensive saris and the ubiquitous scooter. This dowry is usually totally out of proportion to the family's income, so they have to save for this from the day the girl child is born. This is of course disastrous for poor families. The burgeoning urban middle class also engages in this practice, and the parents of educated boys can demand higher dowries from the girl's parents. The dowry requirements are getting higher all the time, with increased consumerism. A car now is now often part of the package. Also, lower caste groups who never used to practice dowry are doing so now, as they also become more consumerist. One politician says, "it is a lethal combination of old values and new wealth – old wine in new bottles".[10] It is estimated that 5,000 new brides are murdered every year by their husbands and in-laws for more dowry. These 'dowry murders' usually are made to appear like accidental kitchen fires or suicides that are hardly even investigated by the police, as they are viewed as mere domestic incidents. Husbands are very rarely convicted.[11] The women's movement have been organising against dowry since the 1970s, which has resulted in the laws being improved to include recognition of dowry-related cruelty and harassment. Their struggle continues, however. Other issues such as health, equal opportunities, domestic violence and rape are also high on their agendas.

The urban middle class do not have to let the pregnancy go full term, because they have access to abortion clinics. For every male foetus aborted, 1,000 females do not make it to birth. Ironically, as modernisation of the economy is creating a 'nouveau riche' middle class in India, traditional attitudes towards girls and women are retrenching rather than loosening. Feminists are predictably divided on the issue of abortion. Agitation in Bombay managed to get pre-natal sex tests banned there, but others argued that this interfered with women's right to control their own fertility. Both groups have women's interests at heart, but express them differently. One doctor who worked in one of Bombay's abortion clinics who was interviewed by Bumiller fully understood this: "If you don't do it, you are creating an unhappy situation for the mother and child. And if you do it, you are discriminating on the basis of sex". The performance of these tests for sex selection is now illegal since the government passed the Prohibition of Sex Selection Act in 2002, but it is still possible to get them in unregulated back street clinics, where a sonograph costs only Rs. 150.[12] Anything is possible in India if you can afford it. One Indian writer comments "though the abominable practices [of female infanticide and dowry] remain because of human weakness, and perhaps human greed, there is general agreement that they are wrong. As a society, we know where we want to be. We just have to get there".[13] It is only when girls and women are given more opportunities to be educated and join the workforce that they can be financially independent, and therefore more culturally valued. So it is a Catch 22 situation.

Getting that elementary education is the next hurdle that Indian girls have to jump. The inequality between men and women is reflected in education statistics. The male literacy rate is 76 per cent, while the female rate is 54 per cent. So only a little more than half of women are literate.[14] In the society that had one of the world's first female Prime Ministers, the limited social role of women is thus inscribed. Even in the late 1980s nearly half of the rural girls between the ages of 12 and 14 did not attend any school for a single day of their lives.[15] This abysmal situation is explained by "cultural factors like son preference, early marriages, inheritance laws and patterns, dowry system, purdah system, and other customs discriminatory to women [making] investment in girls' education very unattractive to the family".[16]

Shashi Tharoor, high-ranking Indian commentator and former UN employee, says that when he is asked the question "what is the single most important thing that can be done to improve the world?" his two-word reply is "educate girls".[17] The education of girls and women has been found to have a whole range of benefits. Girls who have had some schooling are less likely to marry very young and start having children at perhaps the very young age of 14. This is very important because early marriage places young mothers at high risk, as their bodies are not fully mature and ready for childbirth. If they do have children, they are more likely to be more aware of proper health and nutrition for them, improving their survival rate. Also, they are likely to space their children more, therefore ultimately having less children. The World Bank has estimated that for every four years of education, fertility is reduced by one birth per mother.[18] Apart from this, it can also lead to more power in the community in general, as Sen outlines:

> *"There are, in fact, many different ways in which school education may enhance a young woman's decisional power within the family: through its effects on her social standing, her ability to be independent, her power to articulate, her knowledge of the outside world, her skill in influencing group decisions and so on".[19]*

One generally finds that women are ready and willing to learn from each other, be it at community or just family level. It also improves the life chances of the next generation when a mother has had some education. It bears testimony to the old maxim **"if you educate a boy, you educate a person, but if you educate a girl, you educate a family and benefit an entire community".[20]**

When girls do not receive any education, they are treated as unpaid labourers at home and fodder for exploitation as child labourers. Even though of course there are both male and female child labourers, the work done by girl children is all the more invisible because it is often unpaid labour performed in the home. Childminding and fetching water and fuel are almost exclusively girls' jobs. So the ones exploiting girls are usually primarily their own parents. This domestic service is often seen as an alternative to education, as it is perceived as a preparation for their future roles as wives and mothers[21]. There is also the added risk of sexual abuse. These girl child workers are trebly exploited: as females, as children, and as workers.

The sad fact is that the combination of sex discrimination, lack of education, social denigration, malnutrition and disease excludes most of India's women from developing any political agenda, feminist or otherwise. There is a major contradiction between India's legal commitment to equality on the one hand and its modernisation drive on the other, which tends to sharpen the class and gender divide. As is the case with so many aspects of social life in India, they are well aware of the democratic ideal, but they fail dramatically when it is time to put it into practice. In the meantime, NGOs like HOPE plug the gaps in social policy by implementing effective schemes for women's empowerment. A noble example to follow is that of the Self Employed Women's Association (SEWA), in Ahmedabad, Gujarat. This is a combination of a union, a savings bank, a co-op and a training unit that is specifically aimed at women street workers and home-based workers in that area. It has been operational since 1973 and has been a crucial lifeline for underprivileged women in Gujarat.[22]

Practical strategies adopted by these NGOs address the real issues of underprivileged women struggling in harsh cities like Kolkata. Many of the gains made by the women's movement have not touched these women's lives at all, except perhaps that there is more domestic work available in the homes of middle class women. As one feminist author says, "the gains reaped in the name of sisterhood frequently result in the sharpening of class lines by pushing lower-class and minority women further down the socio-economic scale".[23] This individualism is heightened in India because of the persistence of caste bias. As the majority of Indian women's work is in the informal sector, this means that the women involved have no recourse to organising against exploitation. There is no protection from unions against a specific employer. There is no division between the domestic sphere, where they live, eat and sleep, and the public sphere, where they work to earn money. Both are merged into one and everybody must look after her- or himself, without the safety net of a welfare system. When they are given the chance to participate in something like a Self Help Group, it boosts their self-esteem enormously, which in turn improves their level of autonomy and status in their communities. It can show younger women that there are other possibilities rather than just following the well-trodden path of early marriage, large families and dire poverty. Each woman who does something different with her life provides a role model for other women around her, showing them that it is not *natural* that women just live lives of unadulterated drudgery. Also, establishing contact with new networks can help to solve women's problems by providing them with valuable information and resources. In this way, even the poorest of women can be transformed from *objects* to be exploited into *subjects* who can exercise choices and exert some power over their own lives.

1. Empowering Marginalized Underprivileged Women through Self Help Groups (SHGs), Micro Credit, Vocational Training & Income Generation

Meeting of a savings group

Self Help Groups (SHGs), Savings and Micro Credit:

This project aims to empower women through the development of entrepreneurship in their communities. Self-help groups were formed to allow women to save money on a regular basis. The aim of the savings project is to ensure that a fund is available for each woman to allow her to explore an alternative living, having completed a training course in a particular trade. Some of the women are using these savings for their children's education. Loans are also available to these women for business

Life Skills Building, where tailoring and computer training takes place, as well as a café and a craft shop

Arpita Chaudhuri, Co-ordinator of Income Generating Projects

start-up ventures. HOPE runs two vocational training centres for underprivileged women.

Hope Kolkata Foundation, along with MJCC and PBKOJP, has formed SHGs in different slum pockets of Kolkata, where women and children fall victim to chronic poverty and unemployment. Under this project, women SHGs are motivated, trained and assisted in setting up various group ventures. With professional training, these groups acquire skills in finance, raw material procurement, production and the marketing of products. The products are sold at exhibitions where the women are present. Every effort is made to market these products on an ongoing basis so that these women can continue to earn a living within these groups.

The women's savings books

Vocational Training and Income Generation:

This project is an integrated vocational training and income generation programme for underprivileged slum-dwelling women. It is based at the 'Life Skills' building at Panditya Place. The aim of this project is to give every mother and adolescent girl an opportunity to enhance her potential, thereby improving her levels of self-esteem and self-sufficiency. In addition, mothers can carve out quality time for themselves while at the same time earning money to secure better futures for their families. Hundreds of women have been trained in knitting, tailoring, fabric tie and dye, embroidery,

The girls in the tailoring unit

The girls who work in the craft shop

handmade paper craftwork and bakery. After the vocational training, the trainees joined the production unit where they are introduced to an outside local market. They learn how to secure orders, produce materials and products to match those orders and deliver final goods to market. Any profit made is distributed amongst the women.

In addition to this, adult literacy classes are also made available to the women if they so wish. This is but one example of the advantages accrued to women once they have access to education, training and work outside the home. Every woman knows the potential isolation of being a housewife without much outside contact. When an NGO like HOPE throws a lifeline to these women through micro-credit and vocational training, it can make a massive difference to their lives in so many ways.

As well as the ability to earn more income, they are also in contact with others, learning about services available to them and making new friends. They are exposed to things that they otherwise would not have been. It might mean that they might have their families immunised against common diseases where they otherwise might not have, or develop the incentive to learn to read and write, or develop sustainable strategies to improve their lot. It improves the connections between people within communities, and that is always a good thing.

The co-ordinator of micro-finance and income-generating projects is Arpita Chaudhuri (MSW). She and two other social workers go out into the slums and recruit women to join their micro-finance groups. They have 33 groups with about twelve women over the age of eighteen in each. They save money in a bank under a group name. If they need a loan, they can get one if approved by the group. There may be a little internal conflict sometimes, but this is negotiated and managed by the social workers. The women work here for two or three hours in the afternoons, as they often work as cleaners in the mornings. Every year, they make thousands of

Ethel with the girls who have just tailored her purple kurta top

Computer training

Making Christmas cards

Working at the HOPE Café

Christmas cards, which are then sent to the HOPE offices in Ireland and the UK for sale. They can earn up to Rs. 1,000 a month at this work, making a big difference to their family incomes. They have 40 women there at the moment on this programme, which exists since 2007. They give them 'seed money' for small ventures. They also have computer training in the building, a clean, cheerful café and a craft shop where the beautiful goods produced by the women can be purchased.

Profile... Ganga Das

Ganga lives in a slum in Chetla. She is married with two children and in 2005 her husband was involved in an accident that damaged both of his legs, leaving him unable to work. Ganga has had to support the entire family since the accident and found employment as a maidservant. The family did not have sufficient income to provide for their basic needs and the children's education was stopped. In 2007 Ganga joined a self-help group to learn about saving money and currently holds a bank account. Having started to save money she was able to organize the readmission of her children to school and has since secured a permanent job in The HOPE Café. She is now able to provide for her family, care for her husband and support her children in their education.

2. Skills Development

Cricket Coaching for the Development of Underprivileged Childrens' Skills:

This project, spearheaded by PBKOJP, provides a cricket coaching camp for underprivileged children. HOPE's past experience has revealed that although most NGOs work with children, few explore how games and sports can enhance childrens' life experience. This initiative by HOPE involves children putting serious effort into playing cricket, irrespective of age. Like all of the projects with which HOPE is involved, it is holistic in nature. Therefore, It also includes rigorous health check-ups and the provision of proper nutrition. PBKOJP also networks with professional associations, with the hope of securing placements for children within them. To sustain their interest in sports, different tournaments are arranged in which they can to participate. Like children everywhere, this maintains their interest in keeping up regular training.

Workshop & Training on Counselling for Care Givers of Institutional Homes:

While working with disadvantaged women and children, it was noted that rehabilitation was not always possible without psychological therapy. Hence ABWU started a one-year training course in psychological counselling for the caregivers of the shelter homes.

3. Capacity Building Programme for Local NGOs

Development work used to be largely a matter of making decisions based on the technical appraisal of projects. But over the past few years, the Hope Foundation have come to the conclusion that focusing purely on technical programmes while ignoring the organisations that manage them is short sighted and superficial. The result is a consensus that building the capacities of individuals, organisations and institutions is vital for the strengthening of civil society and grassroots development. By increasing the capacity of organisations involved in development, interventions can be made more effective, and their results longer lasting. In response to this need, the Hope Foundation regularly organises capacity building programmes to provide services that empower institutions and individuals to assess their own information needs, set their own priorities and build their own information systems. This programme has been developed in conjunction with the Jayaprakash Institute of Social Change (JPISC), a respected college in Kolkata.

The training programmes have been organised in order to help individual staff members understand the importance of completing tasks within a given timeframe. The programme also encourages staff members to learn to take initiative when responding to the emerging needs of the communities they serve. In addition, the staff members also need to understand their responsibilities better vis-à-vis their beneficiaries. The financial and management skills of local NGOs are also improved. This strengthens the accountability and credibility of local NGOs in the eyes of donors and the community. This in turn enhances confidence, leadership and skills to improve the NGOs' structures, thereby innovating and sharing knowledge and expertise. Negotiation skills are also developed in order to work effectively with government departments and to build alliances, coalitions and networks with other NGOs. This ongoing process will lead to improved efficiency, transparency and accountability in implementing development programmes, and ultimately create an even more enabling atmosphere for the children in HOPE's care.

[1] Luce, 2006, 48-52.
[2] Jayawardena, 1986: 95.
[3] Raju, 2006: 78.
[4] Raju, 2006: 81.
[5] Prasad, 2006: 3.
[6] Baca Zinn & Eitzen, 1999: 124.
[7] Sen, 2005: 228.
[8] Sen, 2000: 106.
[9] Bumiller, 1991: 101-124.
[10] Luce, 2006: 315.
[11] Kumar, 1995: 67.
[12] Luce, 2006: 314.
[13] Prasad, 2006:17.
[14] Raju, 2006: 82.
[15] Sen, 2005:116.
[16] John & Narayan, 2006:190.
[17] Tharoor, 2007a: 165.
[18] Tharoor, 2007a: 165.
[19] Sen, 2000: 218.
[20] Tharoor, 2007a: 165.
[21] John & Narayan, 2006:190.
[22] See www.SEWA.org
[123] Fox-Genovese, 1991: 22.

Conclusion

Extract:

"The rest of the world could learn a lot from India, among which tolerance, the management of diversity and the rooting of democracy in a traditional society loom large. Most people who sample Indian food, music, dancing, literature, architecture and philosophy acquire a lifelong taste for all things Indian. If world trade were to be conducted purely in cultural products then India would have a thumping annual surplus. But India continues to lack in practice – if not in principle – the basic condition of genuine citizenship. Equal citizenship is enshrined in India's Constitution; it is expounded by thousands of academics, journalists, activists and commentators; it is generally presumed to be a reality. But in practice India falls far short of the claims it makes. India's caste system and the traditional mentality of its upper castes are changing and may even be in long-term decline. But they have yet to disappear. As we have seen with the continuation of high illiteracy rates, the low status of women, and the economic valuation of lower-caste children, the persistence of certain traditional attitudes imposes a moral cost on Indian society. Male and female children ought to be seen as priceless. The continuation of such traditions also imposes an economic cost, which India can ill afford to pay".

- **Edward Luce** (2006) *In Spite of the Gods* p.333.

If You Want To Read A Little More…

Involvement with HOPE may be some people's first introduction to India. It really helps enormously to understand their work to do some background reading. Without this, the complexities of Indian life are all the more daunting and perplexing. India has an enormously rich and varied culture and this is reflected in the variety of its literature. Whether in fiction or non-fiction, there is no shortage of literary avenues to explore its many vagaries. The following is a highly subjective and by no means exhaustive list of recommended readings. There are many more besides these but these are the ones that have impressed me so far.

Reading Indian fiction is an accessible means of learning about the major issues that occupy the minds of those who live there. Indian writers, based both in India itself and those from its diaspora community, are to the forefront of contemporary global literature. Some of the world's most exciting authors have emerged from the subcontinent. *Slumdog Millionaire* was the very successful film adaptation of the novel *Q & A* by **Vikas Swarup.** Using the clever technique of structuring the book around answering questions on a TV quiz show, many of the less savoury issues in Indian society are introduced to a wider public. *The Marriage Bureau For Rich People* by **Farahad Zama** is a light-hearted introduction to the issue of Indian parents' searches for suitable marriage partners for their children. A larger tome on the same theme is *A Suitable Boy* by **Vikram Seth**. This is a vast epic family drama set in post-Independence India. Similar themes are ably addressed by **Rohinton Mistry** in two very fine novels. The first is *A Fine Balance* and the second is *Family Matters.* Both of these are highly recommended, as they are very perceptive and insightful explorations of Indian society and culture. *Midnight's Children* by **Salman Rushdie** is a Booker Prize winning novel about a man whose life mirrors that of the Indian itself. **Aravind Adiga** has written two novels that have been highly praised – the Man Booker Prize winning *The White Tiger* and more recently, *Between the Assassinations*, which is very evocative of the southern state of Kerala. *The Peacock Throne* by **Sujit Saraf** is another big read, exploring everyday life and politics in the rat race of contemporary Delhi. On Kolkata, the single best read is of course *The City of Joy* by **Dominique Lapierre**. Backed up by extensive social research, the tribulations of its characters are exactly those faced by that city's real life street and slum dwelling populations. Staying within the region of West Bengal, *The Hungry Tide* by **Amitav Ghosh** is a beautiful rendition of the unique Sundarbans delta area south of Kolkata. *The Inheritance of Loss* by **Kiran Desai** is set in the tea plantations near Darjeeling.

Moving to non-fiction, *Shantaram* by **Gregory Roberts** is an unputdownable description of his time in Bombay, having escaped from an Australian prison. It is an incomparable account of local mafias, slum living and drugs written by a man who apparently has seen and done it all in the Bombay underworld. Numerous travel writers have tackled India, starting with our own heroic **Dervla Murphy**, whose book *On a Shoestring To Coorg* shows young travellers how to do it! Happily, she is still going strong and still travelling. By the way, she is not on Facebook! Her thinking is – if you're away, you're away… *Travels On My Elephant* by **Mark Shand** is his account of his unconventional journey in North East India. The Indian section in **Paul Theroux's** recent book *The Ghost of the Eastern Star* is a perceptive account of his recent time there. Indian-born **V.S. Naipaul** is a harsh critic of his country of birth, no more so than in his *India: A Million Mutinies Now*. When it comes to journalistic accounts of Indian society, one can recommend the writings of **Shashi Tharoor**, who is a highly respected social commentator from Kerala. His two collections - *India: From Midnight to the Millenium* and *The Elephant, the Tiger and the Cellphone* - are very informative and up to date. **Pavan K. Varma**'s *Being Indian* is a scathing critique of power and corruption in contemporary India. Some foreign journalists have been gripped by India over the years. BBC journalist **Mark Tully** was born in Calcutta and has had a lifelong association with India. Of his many books, his *No Full Stops in India* remains a staple read. Scottish born **William Dalrymple** is almost an honorary Indian by now, having lived near Delhi for 25 years. He has written eight books to date on Indian history and society. His book *City of Djinns* on Delhi fills in the background on contemporary life there. His most recent book *Nine Lives: In Search of the Sacred in Modern India* is very highly regarded. **Edward Luce**, a correspondent with the Financial Times, has conducted extensive research in India. His book *In Spite of the Gods: The Strange Rise of Modern India* is highly informative on India's recent development path. For those who wish to delve further into Indian history, *The Wonder That Was India* by **A.L. Basham** could be the first port of call. *Freedom at Midnight* by **Larry Collins** and **Dominique Lapierre** covers the Indian Independence struggle. For contemporary social and economic issues, the work of **Amartya Sen** is a must. Sen, who won the Nobel Prize for Economics in 1998, has produced a vast body of work. His *Development and Freedom* is a highly acclaimed contribution to contemporary social science. It is a very unique blend of economics and philosophy, in which his passion for human rights in India shines through. His collection of writings *The Argumentative Indian* is also very useful.

HOPE Volunteers

An important part of HOPE's support network is the body of volunteers who have worked for them over the years. HOPE is always very grateful for the sterling work done by the volunteers from Ireland and elsewhere. Having raised some money before they leave home, they come to work as teachers in the children's homes, schools and crèches run by HOPE, as well as counsellors, social workers and sports coaches among other things. They are resilient and professional, working tirelessly in this tough old city to help impoverished children and youths.

Arunav Das (Gora), who takes care of office logistics

The main person that helps new volunteers is **Arunav Das**, known as Gora. He is the Mr. Fix It who can solve most issues. It is very common to hear the phrases "ask Gora, call Gora"! In deciding upon one's niche, volunteers are encouraged to put their energy into the most needy projects. They can choose from a variety of activities, and there are always plenty of different jobs to be done. They slot themselves into the schedules run by the very professional local staff. There is great solidarity among the gang of volunteers, with the more established willingly helping out the new recruits and showing them the ropes. Everyone knows that it takes a week or two to find one's feet. Mastering the public transport system, for example, is quite scary at first, but with the support of the others, everybody is hopping on and off buses, autos and taxis in no time. Everybody becomes firm friends, and on weekends there is usually some time to get together socially and relax. Here are some comments from just a few of the HOPE volunteers who were in Kolkata in November and December 2009.

Eoin Fahey

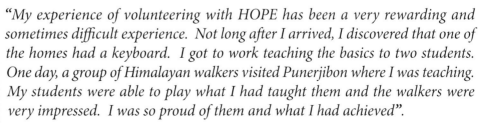

"My experience of volunteering with HOPE has been a very rewarding and sometimes difficult experience. Not long after I arrived, I discovered that one of the homes had a keyboard. I got to work teaching the basics to two students. One day, a group of Himalayan walkers visited Punerjibon where I was teaching. My students were able to play what I had taught them and the walkers were very impressed. I was so proud of them and what I had achieved".

Eoin Fahey, Corofin, Co. Galway – 3 months with HOPE

"Working with the children has been a fabulous experience. I ended up teaching english, maths, crafts and doing a bit of music in four different projects: Arunima (aids hospice), RCFC, HOPE hospital, and Nabadisha. It is amazing how quickly these kids become "your babies". But it's not all rosy. Going out to visit the dump, or seeing babies lying on the street on their own, or realising that when you walk on the sidewalk you are actually walking through someone's homes all pull at the heart strings and sometimes you feel totally helpless but I guess overall I put that into the work I was doing in the schools, in the hope that I was making a difference somewhere. It has been a truly memorable experience and one I will not forget in a hurry".

Michelle Flanagan

Michelle Flanagan, Co. Tipperary - 6 weeks with HOPE

"Kolkata is a city that tests one on every level. The poverty and suffering is undeniable but so is the kindness and warmth of this city's citizens. Nobody should be denied basic human rights - we are all born free and equal. I feel honoured to have had the opportunity to come here with HOPE and to witness first hand the invaluable work that they do".

Kate Cotter

Kate Cotter, Co. Cork, c. 3 months with HOPE

"Life in Kolkata is impossible to describe without actually witnessing it with your own eyes. All I can say is that I'm so grateful for the fact that I'm here as a volunteer and not as a tourist. You have to be prepared to be patient as constructive change only happens gradually but once that does happen the experience can often be deeply fulfilling".

Ben Brooks, Greystones, Co. Wicklow, 4.5 months with HOPE

Alicia Banbury

Mary Gormley

Lindsay Wolford

Ben Brooks

Final Thoughts

It is difficult to sum up the total contribution of the Hope Foundation. It's role in Kolkata and beyond cannot be underestimated. HOPE has saved the lives of thousands of people through its interventions. They are practical and caring in the ways they deal with the minutiae of the needs of the poor.

Kolkata's neglected and abused children and women have a variety of needs. Sometimes it might be a shelter from a violent man, sometimes it might be help in accessing state services, sometimes it might be medical treatment or vaccinations, sometimes it might be a small loan to tide them over a crisis, sometimes it might be a school that will educate their children or sometimes it might be a home for their children when they just cannot cope due to poverty or illness. HOPE provides all of these and more.

It is really only when one sees their homes, schools and clinics with one's own eyes that the magnitude of their work truly sinks in. I hope that, through the words and pictures in this book, I have brought some of that experience to readers who may not be able to visit Kolkata for themselves.

I came across a story in my research for this book that really brought home to me the importance of the quality of the environment in which a child is raised. Sunil Gavaskar is a world famous cricket idol who is known as India's greatest batsman of all time. Considering how crucial cricket is to Indian culture, this is a prestigious position indeed. But it might never have happened. When Gavaskar was born in Bombay in 1949, his uncle came to visit the hospital to see his new nephew. He came again the following day. On that occasion, he noticed that the child in the crib did not have the tiny blemish on his earlobe that he had noticed the previous day. It emerged that the babies had been mixed up and a frantic search ensued for the baby with the correct blemish. He was found in the shack of a poor fisherwoman at the edge of the city, far from the middle class home for which he was destined. The babies were swapped back to their rightful parents and years later, history was made.[1] One wonders what future would have awaited both babies if that uncle had not been so observant.

Each child has a particular package of talents, but unless she/he grows up in a home with parents who are able to nurture and encourage those talents, they might never know their true capabilities. Witnessing the extent of poverty in Kolkata alone, the sheer waste of human potential is staggering. Every child deserves a chance to become what ever his or her talents allow, unhindered by poverty or discrimination. HOPE has provided this chance to thousands of Indian children, whose fate would otherwise have been hunger, illness, addiction, begging, prostitution or quite possibly early death. I spoke to beautiful intelligent young people for whom HOPE has literally been their saviour.

As well as HOPE's everyday work with the children of Kolkata, they continue to be ambitious and are constantly coming up with new ideas to improve and expand their service provision. Led by Maureen's dynamism, they have a daring spirit that drives them, telling them that nothing is impossible and the sky is the limit. They are constantly drumming up new ideas to raise more money and garner more support. They have a huge and ever-growing support network in Ireland and beyond.

Jonathan Rhys Meyers, actor, with pupils from Alexandra College

Freemount National School

Maryfield College

Groups of schoolchildren from all over the country have raised generous amounts of money and visited the projects in Kolkata

The following is a list of the schools whose pupils have participated in the Transition Year Immersion Programme:

- Alexandra College, Milltown, Dublin 6
- Ashton School, Blackrock Road, Cork
- Blackwater Community School, Lismore, Co. Waterford
- Blackrock College, Blackrock, Dublin
- Clonakilty Community College, Clonakilty, Co. Cork
- Coláiste an Chroí Naofa, Carraig Na bhFear, Co. Cork
- Coláiste An Phiarsaigh, Gleann Maghair, Co. Cork
- Coláiste Choilm, Ballincollig, Co. Cork
- Glanmire Community School, Glanmire, Co. Cork
- Hewitt College, Hewitt House, 24 St. Patrick's Hill, Cork
- King's Hospital, Palmerstown, Dublin 20
- Loreto Secondary School, Beaufort, Rathfarnham, Dublin
- Loreto Secondary School, Fermoy, Co. Cork
- Maryfield College, Glandore Rd., Drumcondra, Dublin 9
- Mercy Heights Secondary, Skibbereen, Co. Cork

- Midleton College, Midleton, Co. Cork
- Mount Mercy College, Model Farm Road, Cork
- Mount St. Michael, Rosscarberry, Co.Cork
- Newton School, Newtown Road, Waterford
- Patrician Academy, Mallow, Co.Cork
- Rockwell College, Cashel, Co. Tipperary
- Sacred Heart Secondary School, Clonakilty, Co Cork
- Schull Community College, Schull, Co Cork
- Scoil Mhuire, Wellington Road, Cork
- St. Aloysius College, Carrigtwohill, Co.Cork
- St Angela's College, St. Patrick's Hill, Cork
- St. Brogan's College, Kilbrogan, Bandon, Co. Cork
- St. Flannan's College, Ennis, Co. Clare
- St. Mary's Secondary School, Charleville, Co. Cork
- St. Mary's, Convent of Mercy, Mallow, Co. Cork
- Ursuline Convent, Waterford

Left: Donncha O'Callaghan, Munster rugby player, supporting Anti-Child Labour Day Campaign. Right: Guggi, artist, Amanda Brunker, and Guggi's son, Moe

Mary Kennedy, TV presenter and Gary Kavanagh, hair stylist, attending Dublin Lunch 2009

Many celebrities have also kindly given their time to join the HOPE extended family as Ambassadors in order to raise awareness about their work. Among these are **Donncha O'Callaghan, Jonathan Rhys Myers, Amanda Brunker, Declan O'Rourke, Samina Zia, Christopher Biggins, Mary Kennedy** and **Gary Kavanagh**, as seen in the pictures. Some of the events HOPE have organised include the annual Ball, both in Dublin and in Kolkata, the walkers' groups to the Himalayas and Goa, yoga groups who visit Kolkata, school groups who go to visit the projects, the GT900 Rally for HOPE, the HOPE Golf Classic, as well as a myriad of walks, runs, car boot sales, fasts, garden parties – you name it! There is an event for everyone to take part in! There is also a range of products that can be purchased, from shopping bags to Christmas cards and from hoodies to chocolate and now this book! The Hope Foundation needs all of the support they can get because of the difficulties of the current recession. They can no longer be guaranteed the same support from the

Christopher Biggins, TV personality, with HOPE children

Maureen with Amanda Brunker, model and author, at GT900 Rally 2010

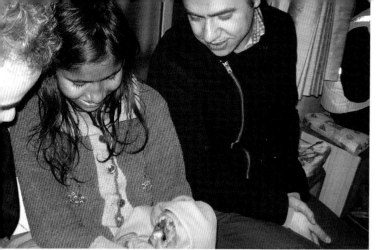

Left: Declan O'Rourke, singer, on HOPE Night Run in Kolkata. Right:Samina Zia, model and former Miss Cork, with HOPE girls in Kolkata

state. At the same time, the children in the homes, schools and clinics in Kolkata still have to be provided for. They cannot be returned to the horror of the streets. **There is simply no option but to keep working for the children, whatever that takes.**

References

Baca Zinn, Maxine & D.S. Eitzen (1999) *Diversity in Families* New York; Longman.

Bales, Kevin (2000) *Disposable People: New Slavery in the Global Economy* Berkeley; University of California Press.

Bose, A.B. (2006) 'Child Development in India' in Council for Social Development *India: Social Development Report* Oxford University Press.

Bumiller, Elisabeth (1991) *May You Be the Mother of a Hundred Sons* New Delhi; Penguin.

Cockburn, Andrew (2003) '21st Century Slaves' *National Geographic* September.

Fox-Genovese, Elizabeth (1991) *Feminism Without Illusions: A Critique of Individualism* Chapel Hill; University of North Carolina Press.

Human Rights Watch (1996) *The Small Hands of Slavery: Bonded Child Labour in India* New York.

Human Rights Watch (2003) *Small Change: Bonded Child Labour in India's Silk Industry* New York.

John, J. & P. Narayanan (2006) 'Elimination of Child Labour: Why Have We Failed?' in Council for Social Development *India: Social Development Report* Oxford University Press.

Kumar, Radha (1995) 'From Chipko to Sati: The Contemporary Women's Movement' in Basu, Amrita (ed.) *The Challenge of Local Feminisms* Boulder; Westview Press.

Lapierre, Dominique (1986) *City of Joy* London; Arrow Books.
Luce, Edward (2006) *In Spite of the Gods: The Strange Rise of Modern India* London; Abacus.
McMichael, Philip (2008) *Development and Social Change: A Global Perspective* Los Angeles; Pine Forge Press (4th ed.).

O'Connell, Brian (2007)'A Steady Flow of Human Traffic' *Irish Times Weekend Review* May 26th.

Patnaik, Utsa (2005) 'Theorising Food Security and Poverty in the Era of Economic Reforms' www.mfcindia.org/utsa.pdf quoted in Patel, Raj (2008).

Patel, Raj (2008) *Stuffed and Starved: Markets, Power and the Hidden Battle for the World Food System* London; Portobello Books.

Prasad, Gitanjali (2006) *The Great Indian Family* New Delhi; Penguin.

Raju, Saraswati (2006) "Locating Women in Social Development" in Council for Social Development *India: Social Development Report* New Delhi; Oxford University Press.

Roy, Rajat (2009) "Pratichi Trust Calls for More Funds to ICDS" Business Standard Dec.24th. (www.business-standard.com/india/news)

Sen, Amartya (2000) *Development as Freedom* New Delhi; Oxford University Press.

Sen, Amartya (2005) *The Argumentative Indian: Writings on Indian Culture, History and Identity* London; Penguin.

Sen, Amartya (2009) "Primary Schooling: I" *The Telegraph* Dec. 19th, p.6.

Shah, Ghanshyam (2004) *Social Movements in India: A Review of Literature* New Delhi; SAGE.

Singh, Shalini (2009) 'India Has Half a Billion Mobiles' *Times of India* Dec. 15, p.10.

Thakur, Pradeep (2009) 'Rising Poverty May Drain Coffers' *Times of India* Dec. 15, p.9.

Tharoor, Shashi (2007a) *The Elephant, the Tiger and the Cellphone: Reflections on India in the Twenty-First Century* New Delhi; Penguin Viking.

Tharoor, Shashi (2007b) *India: From Midnight to the Millenium* New Delhi; Penguin Books.

Theroux, Paul (2008) *Ghost Train to the Eastern Star* London; Hamish Hamilton.

UNICEF (2006) *Judicial Handbook on Combatting Trafficking of Women and Children for Commercial Sexual Exploitation* Geneva.

Varma, Pavan K. (2006) *Being Indian: Inside the Real India* London; Arrow Books.

[i1] Tharoor, 2007a: 237.